FOR BETTER, FOR WORSE, FOR GOD

FOR BETTER,
FOR WORSE,
EXPLORING THE HOLY MYSTERY OF MARRIAGE
FOR GOD

MARY JO PEDERSEN

LOYOLA PRESS.
A JESUIT MINISTRY
Chicago

LOYOLAPRESS.
A JESUIT MINISTRY

3441 N. Ashland Avenue
Chicago, Illinois 60657
(800) 621-1008
www.loyolapress.com

Cover photograph Getty Images, Inc.; rings image © Matthias Kulka/zefa/Corbis
Cover design by Rick Franklin
Interior design by Mia McGloin

Library of Congress Cataloging-in-Publication Data
Pedersen, Mary Jo.
 For better, for worse, for God / Mary Jo Pedersen.
  p. cm.
 Includes bibliographical references.
 ISBN-13: 978-0-8294-2766-0
 ISBN-10: 0-8294-2766-X
 1. Marriage—Religious aspects—Christianity. I. Title.
 BV835.P43 2008
 248.8'44—dc22

                                        2008033488

Printed in the United States of America
09 10 11 12 13 14 Versa 10 9 8 7 6 5 4 3 2 1

CONTENTS

ACKNOWLEDGMENTS

First and foremost, I want to thank my husband, David, whose love for me and dedication to our marriage and whose support for my work with couples is an immense gift.

This book grew out of a series of talks and lectures given at retreats and workshops. I am also grateful to the many couples who have shared with me over the years their own journeys into the mystery of marriage.

I want to thank all my colleagues—theologians, marriage therapists, researchers, and educators—who shared with me their expertise and passion for marriage, helping me bring together the insights of the social sciences with Catholic theology. They have guided and inspired me in my pastoral care of married couples in the Church these past twenty-five years.

The road from retreat to book for this material was a long one. I could never have traversed it without the help of Vinita Wright and Jim Manney, two very talented and patient editors at Loyola Press who walked alongside me tirelessly in order to bring this book to you. I appreciate their writing, editing, and input in helping to create, not just a book about marriage, but a written process for theological reflection on the reader's own lived experience of married life.

1

The Meaning of Marriage
How Can Christian Faith Make a Difference?

I've spent the last twenty-five years working in family ministry and in churches, encountering people in the midst of their joys and struggles as they created family and home. While studying the theology of marriage in graduate school, I also had the opportunity to attend the Smart Marriage conferences sponsored by the Coalition for Marriage, Parenting and Family Education that provided the latest in marriage education and research. As the rich Catholic teachings on marriage and family were unfolded for me in the master's program, I began to see a clear and helpful connection between the Catholic tradition and the insights of marriage therapists and researchers about what makes a marriage healthy and long lasting. It seemed to me that many of the findings from social science research on what makes a satisfying and long-term marriage supported the church's teaching about marriage as a faithful, exclusive partnership for life. My own experience of almost forty years of marriage also bore the truth that our faith, our supportive communities, and our efforts at becoming one flesh and nurturing life together had brought us great happiness and longevity.

In ten years of offering retreats for couples I have found that, for them as well, a belief in God's presence within them individually and as couples gives them a sense of meaning and hope as they face the ups and downs of life together. They recognize the many advantages of married life and the frustrations that are unavoidable. Most of them admit that their spouse is, and is not, the same person they married. Some couples come to these retreats because their marriage has become stale and routine. Other couples have suffered great losses or experienced profound conflicts. Still others come because their life is good and they have a desire for more in their marriage.

This book has grown out of a series of retreats with married couples in which I asked them to reflect on the promises they made at the altar on their wedding day. I hope this book will be a companion for you as you live into those promises and explore the mysteries of married love and commitment. It is designed to engage you and your spouse in a conversation about how your faith influences and transforms your experience of married life. Doing the exercises is as important as reading the text, so I invite you to take your time in reading, pondering, and communicating about the questions—separately, as a couple, or with other couples. **Always do the exercises separately and then together.**

What are the best things about your marriage?

Who supports your marriage?

What originally attracted you to your spouse?

What qualities do you most treasure in your spouse right now?

The Good Marriage

Most couples view marriage through the lens that society offers us. In a "good marriage" the partners have fulfilling jobs, plenty of money, smart and successful children, nice homes and cars, good sex, fun and romance, an active social life, and esteem in the community. These things are admirable and worth working toward. But anyone who has been married more than a short time understands that good marriage must go beyond those aspirations. We may not be able to define what good marriage should be, but we long for it just the same.

In the faith tradition of Christianity, much more is revealed about what marriage really is and about what good marriage is meant to be. Through the lens of faith, marriage is seen as a pathway into the very heart of God where our greatest need for intimacy and belonging can be met. In growing into deeper intimacy and love with one another, couples can find intimacy with the divine. Marriage takes us into the heart of God because marriage challenges us to grow in the self-giving kind of love that is in God's heart, "slow to anger and rich in faithful love" (Psalm 103:8). When we see marriage as the spiritual process it is, we can participate in "ordinary" life with hope and purpose.

The church's view of marriage gives us a *meaning system*, a way to understand marriage as a "school of love" (phrase of Pope John Paul II) and to address some of society's confusion about this great enterprise between God and humankind. The confusion out there is obvious; we are in a marriage crisis. Some 40 percent of first marriages end in divorce, and the rate is higher for second and third marriages. Young people are haunted by the fear of divorce. Failed marriages are common in their experience and many are themselves the children of divorce. They put off marriage until later in life, and, when they do marry, they may view their union as a "trial" marriage. Divorce is only the most flagrant sign of a marriage crisis. Many couples who remain married do so unhappily. They reach a truce with each other. They continue to live together in their disappointment and frustration, and never experience the joy of true intimacy.

Yet God created human beings for love and communion. We are created for intimacy with one another as a pathway to intimacy with our Creator. Though some view the promises of marriage as confining or as curtailing their freedom, the permanence and exclusivity of married love actually free us to achieve greater intimacy with one another. As we grow in love and fidelity, we grow in the likeness of God, in whose image we were created.

What one thing do you know for sure about marriage from your own experience?

As you look at the marriages around you, what lens (attitudes, beliefs, criteria for success) do you use to view them?

The Reality of God's Presence in Your Marriage

When I ask couples for an image that might describe their experience of Christ present in their married life, the responses are rich and varied. In looking back, one couple described God's presence as "the stabilizer bars and seat belts on the roller coaster ride they experienced in their relationship" during a period of crisis.

As Catholic Christians, we engage in *incarnational* thinking. We believe that God lives in us, that God is near in all situations. We even believe that God is present within the relationship of marriage. In fact,

- God is near in place—not only in churches but in kitchens, bedrooms, workplaces, and backyards;
- God is near in time—in good and bad times, in the big and little events and circumstances that make up our lives as a couple and as God's people moving through time;
- God is near in our religious practice—in church traditions and sacraments, in Scripture, in the larger faith community itself, and even in the faith community formed when two people marry and devote themselves to God's purposes as a team of two.

God is actually present in marriage in a unique and very tangible way. *That presence is experienced differently in each couple.* God entered our world in the person of Jesus Christ, taking on human form and sharing the human journey. God does not simply make temporary visits to earth in commonly understood ways such as the sacraments and Scriptures. God makes a home in us, and from within our lives God can be present in the world. And when we are called to the life of marriage, we can be certain that God makes a home in the marital relationship itself.

Read and reflect briefly on Isaiah 43:1–5.

> But now, thus says the Lord,
>> he who created you, O Jacob,
> he who formed you, O Israel:
> Do not fear, for I have redeemed you;
>> I have called you by name, you are mine.
> When you pass through the waters, I will be with you;
>> and through the rivers, they shall not overwhelm you;
> when you walk through fire you shall not be burned,
>> and the flame shall not consume you.
> For I am the LORD, your God,
>> the Holy One of Israel, your Savior.
> I give Egypt as your ransom,
>> Ethiopia and Seba in exchange for you.
> Because you are precious in my sight,
>> and honored, and I love you,
> I give people in return for you,
>> nations in exchange for your life.
> Do not fear, for I am with you;
>> I will bring your offspring from the east,
>> and from the west I will gather you.

We are assured of divine presence in times when we are arguing or not speaking to one another, when we are bored or angry, and when we delight in accomplishments, celebrating the beauty of our children or good times with friends. Place your hand on your heart and feel its rhythmic beating. That is how close God is to you. Nothing we do or experience, however terrible or ecstatic it might seem to us, is ever outside the embrace of God. That is hard for us to comprehend, but it is a truth contained in our understanding of the Incarnation, a deep mystery we see clearly on some days and are blind to on others. In dark times, people often ask, Where is God in this? The real question is this: What is blinding us from seeing the ever-faithful presence of God's Spirit among us?

This particular understanding of how God is with us is unique to the Judeo-Christian tradition. Up until Moses, people understood the gods to be distant and uncaring, even competitive and vindictive about humans. Unlike the capricious Greek or Roman gods of history, our God does not require our cajoling or bargaining. God is not indifferent or harsh or judgmental, even if someone has mistakenly told us that.

God is gracious and kind and merciful, "slow to anger and abounding in steadfast love" (Psalm 103:8). Whatever we may have learned from parents or teachers or fire-and-brimstone sermons, the Judeo–Christian tradition stands behind the truth that God loves us unconditionally, forgives us repeatedly, and stands by us faithfully in every circumstance, even if we do not recognize that presence at the time. The word for this kind of love is *hesed*, translated as "steadfast love." This love takes us beyond our own abilities to love and care for another. This love develops within us patience and kindness and understanding.

This amazing love, which is the presence of God, entered your marriage when you vowed to love one another for better, for worse, forever.

Recall a time, happy or sad, when you were aware of God's presence in your marriage, in an important event, or a decision or circumstance. How was God's presence manifested to you?

We may ignore, but we can nowhere evade, the presence of God. The world is crowded with Him. He walks everywhere incognito. And the incognito is not always hard to penetrate. The real labour is . . . to come awake. Still more, to remain awake.

C. S. Lewis, *Letters to Malcolm*

The Intentional Marriage

When I ask a roomful of married couples whether they have been to a dentist in the past year, most of them raise their hands. If I ask whether they have changed the oil in their cars in the past six months, most respond with a yes. They generally will have updated the virus protection on their computers and made sure their children and pets were current on vaccinations. We know how to take preventative care of our homes and ourselves.

But what about our marriages? When I ask those same couples whether they have gone out on a date together or taken time to talk, or play, or to exclusively spend time together, most admit that there is little regularity or intentionality when it comes to taking preventive care of their relationship.

In *Take Back Your Marriage*, Bill Doherty defines "intentional marriage" as a relationship that does not happen by accident but that the couple consciously keeps choosing to build. Your marriage is an even more important asset than your investments, your house, your car, your business, and other valued dimensions of your life together.

Recent research by Linda Waite and Maggie Gallagher, published in *The Case for Marriage*, shows that married couples live longer, stay healthier, and have happier and more successful children than those who are not married. They earn more money, accumulate more wealth over time, and enjoy more satisfying sexual relationships than those who cohabit, are single, or are divorced. Another way in which marriage is valuable is in the impact it has on children and on others in your community.

And when you made your marriage promises before God, you raised the value of this relationship beyond anything you own. You made these marriage promises to your unborn children, to your extended families, and to the community beyond. The life you are making together has value that cannot be calculated; it is worth your attention and intentions. Caring for this relationship will have an impact far beyond you.

Name something you have done in the past two weeks that has helped preserve your relationship.

Name something you can do to be more intentional about enriching your life together.

2

The Promise

What Did You Say on Your Wedding Day?

On their honeymoon, Paul and Becky had a wonderful romantic time in Cozumel, but during their last dinner in Mexico the conversation drifted to more somber thoughts. If Paul had failed the bar exam, he'd have to take a preparation course right away to get ready to take it again. He'd have to find a part-time job. How much money could he make? Would he have enough time to study? Even if Paul had passed the exam, he'd have to find a job.

This brought up a problem they hadn't discussed much and certainly hadn't settled. Becky wanted to continue to live in or near the Ohio city where they had both grown up and where their families lived. Paul wanted to look for jobs elsewhere as well: Chicago and Washington, D.C. perhaps. They had agreed to put off discussion until "after the wedding." Well, the wedding had been a week ago.

Meanwhile, they worried about money. They'd used a credit card to pay for part of the honeymoon. If Becky's car gave out, as it seemed likely to do, they'd have to take out a loan to buy a new one. Becky was realizing that she was much more worried about money than Paul was. His free-spending ways made her uneasy. Becky hopes that he'll change, now that they're married and must be more careful with finances.

The honeymoon is over. Like every newly married couple, Paul and Becky are embarking on a mysterious journey of discovery and transformation.

> I didn't marry you because you were perfect. I didn't even marry you because I loved you. I married you because you gave me a promise. That promise made up for your faults. And the promise I gave you made up for mine. Two imperfect people got married and it was the promise that made the marriage. And when our children were growing up, it wasn't a house that protected them; and it wasn't our love that protected them—it was that promise.
>
> THORTON WILDER, *The Skin of Our Teeth*

Making the Big Promise

The questions Paul and Becky faced after their honeymoon had to do with what appear to be material issues, such as housing, money, and jobs. But beneath those questions are deeply spiritual issues dealing with the promise to love and honor each other.

The spiritual dimension of marriage is not always easy to recognize in the midst of jobs, household duties, and full calendars. The lens of faith reveals a spirituality woven into the events, relationships, joys, and challenges of everyday life. Your life together is a spiritual journey. The ups and downs, the mistakes and the achievements, the sorrows and the joys—through these things God will form both of you into new people. Marriage is the process through which you can be transformed into a more loving person. It all began with the promises you made on your wedding day.

Recall your wedding day. Go to a quiet place, relax, close your eyes, and think about that day. How did the day begin? How did you feel as you got dressed? What did you look like? What did the church look like when you arrived? Think about some of the details: the flowers, the music, the room where the reception was held.

Recall the people who attended your wedding: your family, the wedding party, friends, special guests who came a long way to be with you.

Chances are, memories of your wedding day will cascade into your mind in a rush of images and impressions. For many if not most people, this day of days, keenly anticipated for years and meticulously planned for months, passes in a rapid blur.

The core of what you did on your wedding day is to exchange vows with your spouse. Here are the words you spoke (or words very similar to what you said). Read them carefully, slowly, and prayerfully. Read them out loud.

The groom says:

I (. . .) , take you (. . .) to be my wife. I promise to be true to you in good times and in bad, in sickness and in health. I will love you and honor you all the days of my life.

The bride says:

I (. . .) , take you (. . .) to be my husband. I promise to be true to you in good times and in bad, in sickness and in health. I will love you and honor you all the days of my life.

What did those vows mean to you then?

In light of your experience of married living, what do those vows mean now?

Understanding What Honor Means

The fact is, we really don't know what it means to be married when we first speak those wedding vows. What we do know is that we said we were going to honor each other.

The promise Paul and Becky made to love and honor "all the days of our lives" ushered them into the mystery of married love. The word *mystery* introduces the marriage rite as the celebrant prays:

> Father,
> You have made the bond of marriage
> a holy mystery,
> a symbol of Christ's love for his Church.

We cannot fully understand (in this life, at least) how marriage can be an image of Christ's love for his church. We cannot fully understand how God enters our lives in a new way when we vow to love and honor our spouse no matter what. But that doesn't mean we can understand nothing of these things. The meaning of the marital mystery gradually becomes clearer as we face the questions and decisions of life together.

On your wedding day you didn't know that you were promising to honor your spouse's love of hours of television sports, or expensive taste in clothing, or snoring, or need for absolute quiet before coffee in the morning. You didn't know it involved persevering through illness, unemployment, heartache over children, or serious disagreement about money. You could not even imagine the joy of your first child's birth or the depth of your own fidelity in hard times. But in facing these challenges, you have the opportunity to be formed—or not—in patience, humility, and selfless love.

In promising to love and honor your spouse, you entered, in a new way, the mystery of God's love. The well of God's steadfast presence is always there for us to dip into. And we're usually most aware of God's presence when things are tough—when we're struggling to control the credit card, when we're trying to decide how to discipline a child, when we're fearful of the implications of a looming job change.

The greatest mystery, and the most comforting truth, is that God is not simply near. God is *here*—in your marriage at all times, not just when things are going well and you are feeling satisfied.

On your wedding day you stood up in front of family and friends and publicly promised to "honor" your spouse. This is an unusual thing to do. Christian wedding ceremonies are the only occasions when someone publicly pledges to honor another person. The promise that "I will love you and honor you all the days of my life" is a radical thing to say. We wouldn't say something like this to an employer or a business partner. Even contractual obligations can be renegotiated. The wedding vows commit us to seek the good of the other person at *all* times, even when times are hard.

Our society is very skeptical about honor. We're more likely to tear down people than to honor them. What does "honor" mean?

Honor means that we treat a person with the respect he or she deserves as God's unique creation. This is easy to do on your wedding day, but it gets harder later on, when you discover that you've married someone who chews ice or talks incessantly or watches television when there's work to do. Nevertheless, this flawed person is your life partner in the great enterprise of married life.

I am reminded of what it means to honor another person when I visit the Benedictine monastery and observe the monks as they gather in church to pray. The monks bow to one another after they bow to the Blessed Sacrament; in this way they acknowledge the presence of Christ in each of them. Though husbands and wives don't bow to each other, they can show honor through their actions and words and by respecting each other's unique qualities and preferences. Honor and mutual respect form the foundation for any partnership, particularly a "partnership of love and life," (one of the memorable terms John Paul II used to describe marriage).

In fact, the differences between husbands and wives deserve special respect. One of the interesting facts I have discovered over many years of working with married couples is that opposites attract. Often we are drawn to another person because he or she possesses qualities that we ourselves lack. A person with an anxious temperament is attracted to someone who is cool and calm. An orderly engineer will connect with an impetuous artist. A deep complementarity lies at the heart of marriage. Men and women are different in many ways, both obvious and subtle, and the differences between us are crucial for a healthy marriage.

Yet these differences often become irritations as the years go by. The calm attitude isn't reassuring anymore; it starts to look like indifference. The impulsiveness that used to be fun and spontaneous is now perceived as annoying. Thus honoring each other's differences can become a challenge. Partners in a marriage usually experience a powerful tendency to wish the other person was more like them. This common temptation in marriage is a classic case of *dis*honoring the other.

A man married eight years commented to me that he felt loved and honored when his wife complimented him or acknowledged his talents in some way. "I don't have to be perfect with her," he said. "She knows I need improvement and she tells me straight out if I'm being a jerk, but I know she loves me as I am anyway. She's straight with me about that too."

On your wedding day you promised to honor your unique, special spouse. That means that you respect and love the person God made, not the person you wish he or she would become, if only they listened to you. This is not simply a matter of social adjustment—it is a spiritual task, one that requires patience, humility, and unconditional love.

Are there persons in your life whom you honor? If so, how do you do that?

What are some simple everyday ways by which you show your spouse that you honor him or her?

Give an example of a time/situation when you felt loved and honored by your spouse.

Vows and Blessings

As Paul and Becky began the practical work of resolving their differences, they did so under the canopy of the nuptial blessings bestowed on their wedding day. After they said their vows to each other, the priest raised his hands and prayed a nuptial blessing over them. You probably don't remember this nuptial blessing in any detail—it's one of the many important things that get lost in the whirlwind of wedding day festivities. But this blessing deserves attention. It expresses the church's view of what you and your spouse just did. It touches on some important aspects of marriage—aspects that will help you participate in this relationship with wisdom and hope.

Here are excerpts from a nuptial blessing that is commonly prayed at weddings today. The blessing prayed at your own wedding might have been slightly different, but the essentials are the same. The italics in these excerpts have been added for emphasis.

You have a mission.

Holy Father, you created mankind in your own image and made man and woman to be joined as husband and wife in union of body and heart and *so fulfill their mission in this world.*

In this part of the blessing, the priest is relating marriage to your mission in life. Marriage is a **vocation**—a way of life to which God calls us. We often hear the word *vocation* used in reference to God's call to the priestly and religious life. But marriage is a vocation, too, having its own mission and way of life, distinct from the priesthood and the single life. When you promised to love and honor your spouse, you were setting out on a path that gives a distinct purpose, shape, and direction to your life in the world.

You formed a covenant.

The celebrant continues the blessing:

> Father, to reveal the plan of your love you made the union of husband and wife *an image of the covenant between you and your people.*

This is the "for better or for worse" aspect of the wedding commitment. The marriage is a **covenant**—a total giving of oneself to another and to God. It is a participation in God's covenant with his people—the covenant that began with the people of Israel and was completed in the new covenant of Jesus Christ. Furthermore, according to the church, your marriage covenant reveals the plan of God's love. There are deep mysteries here, which Paul and Becky can now begin to explore.

You are a sacrament.

> In the fulfillment of this sacrament the marriage of Christian man and woman is the *sign of the marriage between Christ and the Church.* Father stretch out your hand, and bless N. and N.
>
> Lord grant that as they begin to live this *sacrament* they may share with each other the gifts of your love and become one in heart and mind as witnesses to your presence in

their marriage. Help them to create a home together and give them children to be formed by the gospel and to have a place in your family.

A **sacrament** is both a particular manifestation of God's presence and a broad sign of God's presence in our world. God is present in your marriage, and your marriage is a way for God to be present to others. This is true all the time, on your worst days as well as your best ones.

At the beginning of the nuptial Mass, the celebrant refers to marriage as "a holy mystery." Mystery indeed! It seems astonishing that God is present in the cooking and cleaning, the endless chores and the exhausting work, the child rearing and the entertaining, the disappointments and boredom, the frustration and fatigue of marriage. It is amazing to think that our efforts to fulfill these responsibilities reveal God's love for the world. It's a matter of reframing our experience, of looking more deeply beneath the surface of our lives, and of adopting a perspective that reveals the spiritual realities of a committed shared life.

Vocation, covenant, sacrament—these are three great spiritual realities of marriage. Think of them as lenses through which you view your life. These lenses will show you that God's presence is woven through your marriage like brilliant threads in a magnificent fabric.

Who helped shape your view of marriage when you were growing up? What did you learn about marriage by observing or listening to them?

Name one or two things you remember hearing about marriage in your marriage preparation sessions.

Some aspects of a Catholic perspective on marriage are summarized in this chapter. What insight is most helpful to you? Surprising? Challenging?

3

Marriage as Vocation
The Call to Partnered Holiness

When I was in a discussion group with several women religious at a conference in San Francisco, I was surprised by the similarities shared by married and vowed religious participants when it came to the challenges they faced living out their life calling. Both were experiencing times of deep satisfaction and periods of disillusionment. Both loved their communities but struggled with everyday issues of living together. Both were challenged to love more selflessly and to overlook and forgive grievances. Each of us experiences two kinds of callings from God. The first is the universal call to holiness—this we receive in baptism. The second call is determined by our choice of a life path.

We recognize three pathways traditionally chosen by most of the Baptized which refine that universal call to holiness. We call them *vocations* (from the Latin for "to call"). They are: the ordained life (priests and deacons), the single life (including vowed religious), and the married life. Each vocation is a pathway that has its distinct qualities and challenges and many similarities. Each emphasizes a particular aspect of God's work in the world. There's no hierarchy of holiness, with one vocation on top and the others of lesser importance and impact. They work in unison to build God's kingdom. Each of them offers numerous opportunities to share in the dying and rising of Christ and to do his work in the world. Holiness is the work of the Holy Spirit in us as we take advantage of the opportunities that marriage gives us to be like Christ.

When you send a wedding gift or greet a bride and groom in the receiving line, you usually wish them much happiness. You probably don't think to greet the new couple with a wish for much holiness. But this would be a fitting wish. Christian marriage is a pathway to holiness. The path that leads from the altar to the kitchen table is regarded by the church as a vocation, a call to grow in holiness together as husband and wife in communion with each other and with God.

When you are married, you are no longer alone on life's journey to holiness. At your wedding, God joins you together and underwrites your vows of fidelity with his own steadfast love. Though you remain a unique individual before God, in marriage you journey this world as "one flesh." Married living brings the joy and comfort of belonging to another and the adventure of growing into a new family together. Married living, like the other vocations, calls us to patience and forgiveness, to compassion and selflessness, to wholeness and holiness.

What Holiness Is—from Baptism to Marriage

Sit down with your spouse at a table with pen and paper. Say the word *holy* and write down the images, ideas, and people that come to mind.

I've asked many hundreds of couples to do this exercise. The notions of holiness they record tend to fall into certain categories. Holiness is strongly colored by images of sacred places separated from the world: monasteries, quiet and empty churches, places of magnificent (and silent) natural beauty that elevate the heart to prayer. Many people think of holy objects: a crucifix, a chalice, votive candles, a tabernacle.

Our ideas of what kinds of people are holy are influenced by the stories of saints and martyrs and their heroic activity. Holy people undertake long periods of prayer. They might fast strenuously. They spend hours reading Scripture and writing spiritual books. Holy people do outstanding things such as give up their lives or tirelessly work with the poor and needy.

Holy people are saints: Joan of Arc, Francis of Assisi, Francis Xavier, Mother Teresa—men and women who have performed such great deeds for God that the church remembers them and holds them up for the rest of us to imitate.

These notions of holiness are true and inspiring, but they are very incomplete. What is missing is a sense of the everyday-ness of holy living. You may occasionally get away on a retreat for a weekend of quiet prayer, and you may have the opportunity to do some significant work of service. But the ordinary way to holiness for most married persons is—well, *ordinary*. Sometimes it feels heroic, but usually it's not.

Married holiness is made up of acts of virtue and faithful choices such as giving up tickets to a big football game in order to attend your in-laws' anniversary celebration. Mother Teresa said that holiness consists of doing ordinary things with extraordinary love; simple things like cooking a meal or cleaning up a big mess.

Everyone who has been baptized has received what the church refers to as a universal call to holiness. The pouring of water over the baptized person's head during the baptismal rite signifies the Christian's dying and rising with Christ. The preferred ritual of adult baptism makes this point with special clarity. The new Christian is fully immersed in water; this reenacts dying with Christ. Then the Christian arises from the water; this symbolizes our share in the resurrection of Christ.

The ups and downs of married life provide countless opportunities to experience the spiritual dynamic of dying and rising with Christ. Disappointments and achievements, losses and victories, sadness and joy are woven into the fabric of married life. Through these challenges and experiences, love is perfected and we are transformed.

In the sacrament of baptism, the new Christian is anointed with oil. This symbolizes being set apart for special service to God in the world. In fact, the word *holy* comes from a Greek word meaning "set apart." But we are not set apart because we are better than others. We are set apart in the sense that we have a calling to assist in building God's reign on earth. Marriage is not just for ourselves; it is for others as well.

Share with your spouse how the call to holiness is present for you:

- When forgiveness is needed
- When radical acceptance of your spouse is required
- When you serve the needs of your spouse or family member
- When you are called to give of yourself for the good of the other

---

Spiritual Disciplines in Marriage

Dan and Ashley work alternate shifts so as to avoid the cost of child-care. When Dan comes home at the end of the day, usually he's very tired and is ready for some quiet decompression time. Instead, he practices what I call "doorway patience." He walks through the door and the kids descend on him, clamoring for his attention. Ashley, who is working an evening shift, needs time to get herself ready as well as complete dinner. After talking over the tension surrounding dinner time, Dan began to consciously put his own needs aside for a half hour or so to help with dinner and the children, instead of going to the bedroom to change and watch the evening news.

It's no easier for my friend to practice doorway patience than it is for a monk to get out of bed at sunrise for morning prayer. Each is a spiritual discipline characteristic of that person's vocation. Doorway patience and morning prayer are both ways of loving and serving God. They both cost something, and they are both ways to die to yourself in order to give life to community.

Though there are heroic moments in marriage, the path to holiness for couples is the path of the everyday dying to self. This path is shaped by a promise to love and honor each other forever. It involves making money, making love, and making a home. It means adjusting to a spouse's idiosyncrasies, wiping a baby's bottom, caring for sick parents, organizing a family vacation, and fretting in the wee hours of the morning because your teenager isn't home.

In Matthew's Gospel Jesus tells the parable of the last judgment, where the saved receive an eternal reward because they fed the hungry, clothed the naked, cared for the sick, and sheltered the homeless. That's the very definition of what couples do for each other and what parents of dependent children do, day in and day out. The average American family is five mortgage payments away from homelessness. That's why faithfully going to work every day is an act of love that shelters those who would otherwise be homeless. Parents feed the hungry—hungry kids and their friends, each other, friends and neighbors in need of a good meal. They care for the sick all the time—sick children, ill spouses, infirm parents and neighbors. These are very ordinary things, but when couples do them out of love, they are quite literally doing the work of God.

Go back to that paper on which you wrote down your images and ideas of holiness. Now expand your thinking. Think of the ways in which you customarily serve your spouse, your children, your family members, and neighbors. Consider what you do even "for the least of these." Think of how you accept your spouse, forgive your spouse, and love your spouse unconditionally. Now add these acts of holy service to your list.

The path of the ordinary is not glamorous. Those who walk it rarely stand out, and they are seldom recognized. The path of the ordinary, walked in love and fidelity, is a humble path, but it's a holy path.

The call to holiness in marriage is not limited to what we do. It includes how we *are* with each other. It is a call to radical acceptance of a spouse as he or she is, a call to forgive over and over again, a call to be faithful in good and bad times. The pathway of holiness is unique for every couple. At one time the call is to be strong in adversity, at another time to be vulnerable in communicating our needs.

Marriage is not for the faint of heart! Like all vocations, marriage requires particular spiritual disciplines to accomplish its goals. My friend's "doorway patience" is an example of what's required. Such actions literally "make love" happen in the world, and that is a holy thing to do.

Most people associate spiritual disciplines with monastic communities or religious life. Spiritual disciplines are practices that deepen our relationship with God and with the community in which we live. Such actions, attitudes, and practices make us more open to the power of the Holy Spirit, who can make all things holy—things as simple as bread and wine and even actions as ordinary as cooking special meals for a diabetic spouse.

Spiritual disciplines help form and transform each of us so that we can accomplish our mission. Prayer, fasting, and giving of our various resources are spiritual disciplines encouraged for all vocations. It's easy to visualize how those spiritual disciplines are at work in monastic communities as one thinks of them rising early for prayer and following the rubrics of community life. But you seldom hear people talking about the spiritual disciplines of the home because the disciplines of the home are neatly folded into daily and often humdrum activities.

The mission of the family, of which marriage is the center, is to become "an intimate community of love and life." So the disciplines of marriage are ones that help couples become an intimate community or that help them love more and create and serve life better in their home life and beyond.

What spiritual disciplines have been required of you in your experience of marriage?

Becoming One Flesh

The pathway to holiness in marriage is unique for each couple, depending upon their situation with work, extended family, children, and the community. But all couples share one particular challenge that ordained, consecrated, and single persons do not face. That is the challenge of "becoming one flesh" with another person for life.

Go back to that moment in church, as you and your spouse stand nervous and smiling in front of family and friends. Every vocation has a beginning point; this moment is yours. The outstanding fact about it, and the quality that defines it until one of you dies, is that it's a journey you will take *together*.

No other vocation requires becoming one flesh with another person. It's a struggle that will be the source of your greatest joys, greatest accomplishments, and greatest frustrations. The union of man and woman is at the heart of the vocation of marriage—God designed it that way.

The book of Genesis says that, at the very beginning, God created human beings both male and female, and that is why "a man leaves his father and his mother and clings to his wife, and they become one flesh." (Genesis 2:24) The desire that men and women feel for each other is satisfied in marriage. In their communion with one another, couples are a reflection of God's desire for union with humankind, the work of his hands. In the Gospels, Jesus says, "I am the vine, you are the branches. Those who abide in me and I in them bear much fruit." (John 15:5)

Our first ideas of becoming "one flesh" usually focus on sex. The sexual union of man and woman is indeed important, and we will reflect on that in later chapters. But becoming one flesh means more than a physical union. Genesis says that God created man and woman to become one body. The Hebrew word for body, or "flesh," refers to the physical body for sure, but it encompasses much more. *Body* includes the whole person: body, mind, and spirit. We're called to be united with our spouse physically, emotionally, and spiritually while retaining our unique individuality. God's design for this partnership is that it nurtures our lives and in so doing gives life to the world.

Men Are from Mars and Women Are from Venus—John Gray and his publishers picked a great title for his bestselling book on marriage. It has become a popular shorthand way of saying that men and women are profoundly different. They are so different that it often seems they live on different planets.

In addition to the obvious anatomical differences, men and women are "wired" differently in their communication styles, emotional makeup, and sexual responses. You and your spouse differ as individuals. Your temperaments are different. You come into marriage with dissimilar expectations, desires, hopes, and approaches to problem solving. And while you don't really live on different planets, you come from different places. You were raised in different families. Your family of origin gave you ideas about marriage, child rearing, sex roles, and family values that are different from your spouse's. Some marriage experts say that incompatibility was never a valid reason for divorce because all couples are incompatible to some extent.

Creating an "us" in the face of these differences is a challenging dimension of the vocation of marriage. To become "one," partners must understand the many ways in which they differ from each other and recognize how their differences can work in their favor in terms of their partnership. They also need to learn to manage these differences without hurting each other.

First, becoming an "us" is a realistic goal. The differences between men and women are great, but the desire to achieve unity is even greater. Men and women deeply desire each other; most men and women want to share their lives with a partner of the opposite sex. We see this powerful attraction between the sexes in all of nature. A male emperor moth can detect a female emperor moth seven miles away. A yearning to be one seems to be hardwired into our beings. If God created us this way, we can be assured that he gives us the grace to achieve the union we desire.

Second, the work of becoming an "us" is spiritual work, and it requires spiritual disciplines, as already mentioned. Each vocation has its distinctive challenges, and becoming one with a particular other person for life is the unique challenge of marriage; the spiritual disciplines of marriage are the tools we use to achieve it. The disciplines we practice within marriage may seem mundane, such as counting to ten before returning an angry response, or waiting patiently for a spouse who is slow, but they accomplish something remarkable. They allow us to live in communion with someone who feels, perceives, reacts, responds, and loves differently from us.

Living in communion is holy because the conjugal life both mirrors and provides the world with an experience of belonging and acceptance God desires with us. Like the "communion" we experience in the sacrament of Eucharist, marriage can provide the opportunity to "be one in Christ," the goal for all baptized believers.

When have you put your own needs/convenience/desires aside for the good of your spouse or family?

In what way does that action contribute to a sense of communion or one-ness among you?

A vocation is both an invitation from God and our response to this call. It is an invitation to live a certain kind of life, one shaped by two powerful influences; the values of Christian faith and the gifts that we find in ourselves.

JAMES AND EVELYN EATON WHITEHEAD,
in *Marrying Well*

Balancing Togetherness
with Individuality

An important spiritual discipline for a couple is finding a point of balance in their relationship between togetherness and individuality. Union in marriage does not mean the destruction of each partner's individuality. Differences are actually an advantage to a partnership. The goal in Christian marriage is to become a partnership of equals in which each spouse respects and protects the other's unique identity. After all, it's our differences that attracted us to each other in the first place.

Tom and Bea are a good example. Bea is spontaneous and loves to explore new places and ways of doing things. She is a "carpe diem" person, living every moment to the fullest! Tom likes the comfort of familiar places and is quite methodical in the way he does things. He's good at long-range planning, takes few risks, and wants to know ahead of time if there is a change in the routine. As individuals, they experience the frustration of differing styles. But as a couple they make a great team balancing out one another's excesses. She makes sure they're not in a rut, and he provides a sense of security for their life together.

Many cohabiting couples need reassurance about this point because they fear they will lose their identity if they get married. Contemporary society values autonomy and independence over the common good and solidarity with another. One secret of satisfying marriages is the partners' ability to balance individual freedom with a commitment to their relationship.

In fact, contemporary marriages can become unbalanced toward independence. Husband and wife will live as separate individuals with their own friends, hobbies, interests, careers, and checking accounts. This kind of marriage is stuck in the stage of adolescence. Men and women who jealously guard their individuality resemble a teenager's relationship with parents. The adolescent works at being different from the parents in order to create a self. He or she will often deliberately do the opposite of what the parent wants in order to strengthen their sense of separateness. This is normal for a teenager (though it can be excessive, making it hard for parents to live with). It is not a healthy attitude for mature married spouses who consider themselves equals.

The opposite imbalance is the dependent marriage. Sometimes the two partners will attempt to meld their individual identities into a "marriage" identity. They will do everything together, spend all their free time together, and become jealous of each other's friends and activities. These couples tend to neglect developing their unique gifts and interests. At times, one partner will become dependent on the other. The dominant partner will set the direction for the marriage, take the lead in social and financial matters, direct the children, and otherwise make all the decisions. This kind of marriage is childlike, similar to a young child's relationship with a parent. The child identifies with the parent and resists becoming his own person. Such a couple can hardly achieve mutuality, which is a first step toward becoming a "partnership of love and life."

The point of balance is an *interdependent* marriage that fosters communion and a healthy "us." This is a marriage in which the partners enjoy a rich and satisfying common life while maintaining their own interests, opinions, and feelings. Each partner recognizes and honors the other's individuality. In fact, each shares his or her unique self with the other. The differences between them have become part of their common life. In an interdependent marriage, the partners do not always need to feel the same way or like the same things in order to feel close to each other. They can appreciate and understand each other's thoughts and feelings and make compromises when necessary for the common good. This is what it means to honor one another and to create a healthy "us."

In modern writings of the Catholic tradition, marriage is seen as a partnership of men and women equal in dignity and value. Equality does not mean sameness. Because spouses have different skills and abilities, they are able to fill the necessary roles and duties of marriage according to their strengths. A wife may be better at money management; a husband might be better at scheduling and planning. She might like to garden and do things to brighten the home and yard. He might be a savvier shopper with a better eye for bargains. These are examples of how complimentary roles can work in an interdependent marriage.

Pope John Paul II used the term *mutuality* to describe this respectful balance in marriage. Mutuality is a rare human achievement in any relationship, requiring profound respect and appreciation for the gifts and strengths of the other. More challenging yet, it requires a level of vulnerability that allows one to relinquish control of something for the sake of the common good. Achieving mutuality in marriage is both an accomplishment and a lifelong task.

Not all Christian teaching about marriage recognizes the importance of mutuality. Two attitudes in particular actually work against it. One is the idea that the woman has primary responsibility for nurturing the couple relationship. The other is the notion that the husband has the role of spiritual "headship," or leadership, in the marital union. These ideas are often promoted by fundamentalist Christians, and they run counter to the Catholic teaching about the radical equality and mutuality of marriage. Husband and wife *both* submit to each other, and together they submit to Christ. In a marriage of equals there are seasons during which one person takes a more prominent role, whether in leadership or in nurture, depending on what is happening in their life. Both share responsibility for the marriage. Both are challenged to love as Christ loves us—selflessly and unconditionally.

Most marriages go through phases of the partners being too independent (adolescent) or too dependent (childlike). Where do you see your marriage on the spectrum?

Give an example of how you operate as interdependent partners in your marriage.

Different people require different mixes of independence and mutuality and the mix may need to be re-negotiated from time to time. "You do your thing and I'll do mine," if allowed to be the keystone of the relationship, means you no longer have a relationship.

The Friendship Factor

Personality Differences

George is a "thinker" husband married to Kate, a "feeling" wife. They are discussing where they will go for their anniversary. George has collected lots of data about costs, distance, activities, and services available at a resort. He has summarized this data on a legal pad, and he sits down with Kate to make some decisions. Kate doesn't even look at George's data. She is worried about the length of time they will be away from their children. She's concerned about what others might think of their lavish plans. She wants to talk to George about these worries. As for where to go—all Kate wants is a quiet and romantic place where they can spend some quality time together.

George is coming from Mars and Kate from Venus. To peacefully plan their getaway, they need to meet on Earth in the real world of their marriage. Each needs to acknowledge the value of the other's approach to the planning process. Each needs to listen patiently to the other's concerns and desires. Both must be willing to compromise a bit. If they do these things, they will strengthen the "us" that they have been building since the day of their marriage.

Each of us finds that certain ways of thinking and acting are easier than others. Some of us are extroverts; we like parties, social gatherings, conversation, and having lots of people around. In fact, we are energized by the presence of others. Some of us are introverts; we like quiet, solitude, and introspection. We recharge our energies by time alone.

Some people make decisions by carefully lining up all the facts and systematically reviewing alternatives. Others quickly look at the choices and make a decision based on what "feels right." Some people like a way of life that is orderly, predictable, and stable. Others find this dull; they want spontaneity, variety, even a touch of chaos.

When choosing a mate, most people are attracted to some degree by their opposite. People of different personalities and temperaments are fascinating to be with. The introvert's world is broadened by the extrovert's social network. The spontaneous risk taker finds a sense of security in the company of a disciplined list maker.

I am a very extroverted and feeling person. I love to be around people; I draw energy from crowds. I express my feelings openly, and I am exquisitely sensitive to the feelings of others. But when I was dating, I was constantly attracted to men who were the strong, silent, thinking type. Men who were like me—extroverted, life-of-the-party types—wore me out. I felt more comfortable with quieter men. I found a very good one and married him. Soon, like most couples, we were confronted with the daunting task of making a common life with someone who thinks and acts in a different way.

These personality differences are a source of strength in marriage. I like to think that when our strengths and limitations are put together that we function like one pretty well-rounded person. But differences are also the source of much irritation. If we don't honor the unique temperament of our spouse, these differences can become the source of serious conflict and a gradual breakdown of affection.

Steve and Meghan are friends of ours who came into their marriage with very different tastes in entertainment. Meghan is a serious devotee of ballet and opera. She loves to go to live performances whenever she can. Steve is a devoted football fan. He has season tickets to his favorite college team and spends Sunday afternoons watching football on television. Each of them is bored by the other's pastime. After they were married, they pursued their interests separately. Soon they were spending their leisure time apart: Meghan at the opera house with a friend, Steve with his buddies in the stadium or in front of the TV.

When they recognized their gradual drifting apart, they decided to try taking an active part in the other's recreational pursuit. Meghan went to some football games. She read *Football for Dummies* and watched some games with her husband on Sunday afternoons. Though she couldn't always follow the action, she grew to enjoy watching her husband's excitement and his ability to relax, laugh, and cheer his teams onward. For his part, Steve began going to the ballet and opera with his wife several times a year. Before going to an opera she would read him a synopsis of the plot. Once he understood something of what was going on onstage he began to enjoy it. Steven and Meghan still prefer their different interests. But the compromises gave them the recreational time so necessary for a healthy "us." As Steve once jokingly put it, "*I* don't like ballet, but *we* like ballet."

Steve and Meghan are not two people living their separate lives in the same house; they are building a shared life that is rich and satisfying. It's a good example of the hard work of becoming one flesh, of two "I"s becoming an "us."

When we speak about the spiritual discipline of balancing individuality with togetherness, we recognize that self-respect and self-denial are both part of the process of achieving communion. Sometimes we get what we want, and sometimes we bow to the desires of the other. Balancing on this tightrope is more than a psychological exercise; it is a gradual and profound spiritual transformation requiring self sacrificing love.

Reflect for a moment to yourself about what personality traits most attracted you to your spouse. Share those traits with your spouse and talk about whether they represent similarities or differences between you.

Name a difference in personality / temperament that is good for your marriage. Name a difference in personality / temperament that causes conflict. How do you or can you honor those differences?

Gender Differences

As you create a life together, you and your spouse are likely to encounter a second set of challenges to becoming one in mind and heart. This is the fact that men and women are "wired" differently. To some extent, people do seem to think, act, and communicate differently by virtue of their gender.

First, some disclaimers and warnings. Research on gender differences isn't always clear and it's often controversial. Statements such as "women are more nurturing" and "men are more aggressive" are broad generalizations. There are many nurturing men and aggressive women. Furthermore, these kinds of statements can be used to support sexual stereotypes that are quite damaging (as well as inaccurate), especially if they influence child rearing. Finally, the "nature-nurture" debate isn't resolved. It's very difficult to say with scientific precision that men and women behave in a certain way because they are "born that way." Culture and socialization play a role too.

Nevertheless, gender differences do exist. In general, men seem to have a propensity to face and solve practical problems. When faced with a tangled or difficult situation, men are more interested in finding a solution. They are less interested in the emotions surrounding the problem. Women score higher than men on tests measuring agreeableness, that is, a tendency to be compassionate and cooperative. In general, they are seen as more empathic—able to express concern about others and to connect with them emotionally.

A good example of gender differences is the different male and female response to the problem of being lost. For a man, being lost is a problem that he needs to solve. He will try to figure out the solution himself long after the woman is ready to seek assistance. For a man, finding his way is a personal challenge. Asking for help puts him "one down" in a power hierarchy in which knowledge is a form of power. On the other hand, women don't mind asking for directions because this is a helpful transaction. Women feel closer to a person who has given them helpful information. For many men, knowledge is power, whereas for women, gaining knowledge or information is an opportunity to connect with others.

Some of the most interesting gender differences concern dissimilar communication styles. In her book *You Just Don't Understand: Women and Men in Conversation*, the linguist Deborah Tannen has studied the way men and women talk. These are some of the differences she found:

- Men engage in *report* talk: they exchange information. Women more readily engage in *rapport* talk: conversation with the purpose of connecting with someone.
- Men tend to talk more than women in public situations, but women tend to talk more than men at home.
- Girls and women tend to talk at length about one topic, but boys and men tend to jump from topic to topic.
- When listening, women make more noises such as "mm-hmm" and "uh-huh," while men are more likely to listen silently.

Tannen is describing something that millions of married couples know very well. It's the stuff of marital jokes, but also the seeds of something that can undermine marriage. The wife desires intimacy with her husband by talking to him. She connects to him that way. For the husband, conversation is an information exchange. He reports the day's events and is finished. He wonders why his wife wants to keep talking. Here is the source of the familiar stereotype of the troubled marriage: the union of the talkative, high-maintenance woman and the remote, emotionally distant man.

Intimacy comes with the work of appreciating and working with differences such as these. It is the work of becoming an "us." This is a spiritual discipline. In our radical acceptance of another person *as he or she is*, we are imaging the God who loves us unconditionally. It is also a spiritual discipline at the same time to gently challenge our spouse to needed change. These spiritual disciplines transform both the one who practices them and those who receive the gift of unconditional acceptance.

Think for a moment about the gender differences that exist in your own relationship.

In what ways are you personally enriched by the gender differences of your spouse?

Think of a time when you have effectively accomplished something together—completed a task, made a decision or dealt with a situation. What individual/gender strengths did you pull from to succeed?

Family-of-Origin Differences

Marriage experts quip that the three leading sources of conflict in marriage are time and money, sex, and in-laws. These stand for larger issues. "Time and money" denote a whole host of questions: what lifestyle will the family have? How will we balance work and home time? What sacrifices will be made to advance the partners' careers? "Sex" refers to a host of attitudes and activities that cultivate intimacy in the broadest sense, not merely how often the couple will make love. "In-laws" stands for the challenge of coming to terms with the differences in the way you were raised and in the personalities and behavior patterns of extended family.

Most of us already understand that the way we were raised has a profound impact on our psychological, emotional, and spiritual makeup. Children from happy, well-adjusted families tend to grow into happy, well-adjusted adults. The reverse is also true: emotional problems, addictions, fears, and relationship difficulties can often be traced to problems we had growing up.

We bring these emotional issues into our marriages. But here I want to focus on a particular subset of these issues. That is the way in which the habits, attitudes, and assumptions about life that come from our family of origin complicate our efforts to create an "us" and a new family with a partner who was raised differently.

Perhaps an example will help. Anna was raised in an Italian family where parents and children freely and openly expressed emotions, both positive and negative. They didn't mind heatedly disagreeing with each other. They were quick to make up. Family gatherings were marked by hugging and kissing, boisterous talk, and noisy meals. The women in the family "took care" of the men. The paramount family virtue was loyalty. Family members stood together against any kind of criticism from the outside.

Anna married Pete, who came from a Danish family. Pete grew up in a quiet home where people seldom raised their voices. Parents and children were reluctant to openly express feelings or complaints with each other. When they did, they tried to keep emotion out of the discussion. Arguments were like debates conducted in a proper manner. Family members were loving but not affectionate. The paramount virtue was responsibility.

At home, Anna worked hard to take care of Pete's personal needs, even though both had full-time jobs. She dropped off and picked up his dry cleaning, made his dental appointments, supervised his schedule, and had dinner on the table when he came home from work. This was the way she was raised; her mother took care of her father in the same way. With time she began to feel resentful at this arrangement. She felt burdened by the extra work she was doing. For his part, Pete couldn't understand why his wife seemed snippy and upset at dinnertime. It bothered him, but he didn't want to say anything about it.

She needed a rousing argument to clear the air. He preferred an unimpassioned debate. She thought they should go to dinner at her parents' home every Sunday because her parents expected it. He was upset that such an expectation monopolized their weekend.

The source of these problems lay in the culture of the families Anna and Pete were raised in. They grew up thinking that their particular family culture was normal, the way families were supposed to be. Some couples move far away from their families to avoid such conflicts, robbing their children and themselves of the love and support provided by extended family. With time, healthy couples eventually learn that there are other ways to be a married couple within extended family, ways that are more satisfying to them. Negotiating those differences over holidays, at weddings, birthdays, and on a daily basis demands maturity and the virtues of charity and prudence. The exercise of these two virtues is equally difficult for the monk in community as it is for the spouses in extended family. Both practice charity and prudence for the common good of the community.

Name some ways in which your families of origin are different from each other—in their attitudes about holidays, expressions of affection, traditions, money, and so forth.

Give an example of how you have negotiated family of origin differences that have helped you form an "us."

Doing the Work of Oneness

Sing and dance together and be joyous, but let each one of you be alone,

   Even as the strings of a lute are alone though they quiver with the same music.

—KAHLIL GIBRAN, *The Prophet*

The hard work of oneness has a meaning and significance far greater than it seems to have at first glance. Recognizing and dealing with the differences between you and your spouse is, first of all, *work*. It's practical, time-consuming, meticulous work in the kitchen, bedroom, and garage. But it's also *creative* work. It's a process of personal transformation. Sometimes you change. Sometimes you are the catalyst for change in your spouse.

This is the work of creation. In marriage we can see an active, inventive, dynamic God at work, transforming husband and wife and creating something that never existed before. Our part is to recognize what needs to be changed. Sometimes we will die to ourselves and let go of something that we value. Sometimes we challenge our spouse to relinquish or modify a cherished trait or habit. Sometimes we wait patiently. The Vatican II document *Gaudium et spes* calls marriage "an intimate partnership of life and love." It's not a perfect partnership—but an intimate one.

Even the most loving couples who have years of experience at becoming an "us" acknowledge that there will always be some distance between spouses. The metaphor that Kahlil Gibran uses for marriage addresses this distance. "Stand together yet not too near together; for the pillars of the temple stand apart, / And the oak tree and the cypress grow not in each other's shadow"

(Gibran, p. 17). Some distance between spouses allows both to keep growing and changing in response to the lessons life is offering. Sometimes when a person wants to end a relationship he will say something like, "She's not the person I married"—as if this were a bad thing! Yet any healthy person grows and changes. After thirty-five years of marriage, couples often remark that just when they think they have their spouse figured out, he or she changes and begins to do or think about things differently. Couples who honor the space between them allow each other to continue growing and changing in response to life and God's work within them. Making room for being alone, better yet, for solitude is a gift each spouse can give to the other.

In a partnership in which solitude is respected as a companion to intimacy, each spouse is freed of the fear of losing one's self. One mysterious aspect of married love is that two people can give themselves to one another without giving away their identity. Solitude is a healthy aspect of human life and growth. Being comfortable with being alone is a sign of self-knowledge and self-acceptance. In accepting ourselves as we are, with both gifts and limitations, we can more freely give of ourselves to others. Solitude reminds us of our need for God. Unlike loneliness, which gives us the feeling of being abandoned, solitude can foster a sense of belonging to a greater whole.

A woman once told me that although she was happy in her marriage, she experienced periods of feeling very much alone. This is not unusual, even for happily married couples. The rhythm of growth in marriage includes feelings of both separation and profound unity. That distance is unavoidable and is part of the unique rhythm of healthy partnerships. Mature married love honors the inimitable singularity of each spouse; this kind of love doesn't seek to absorb the other in the self or to be absorbed in the other. It wants the object of love to be him or herself—to be other. The distance between spouses is fertile ground for growth and like the fallow fields, allows for new life and growth in the relationship.

The truth is that we will never become perfectly one in our marriages. Partners in a marriage will always retain their individuality, and that means there will always be differences between husband and wife. Every person is a mystery of sorts—a mystery we can never know completely. There will always be something new and surprising to learn about the person that we know intimately. The imperfect oneness that we achieve in marriage is only a foreshadowing of the perfect union that God has prepared for us in the life to come.

Name some ways in which you honor the distance between you.

How do you respond when the distance is not respected?

On a scale of 1–5, how comfortable is each of you with the experience of solitude? How can you nurture periods of solitude without experiencing lonliness?

What is helpful in determining how much distance is healthy and how much is unhealthy avoidance of each other?

A good marriage is that in which each appoints the other guardian of his solitude. Once the realization is accepted that even between the closest of human beings infinite distances continue to exist, a wonderful living side by side can grow up, if they succeed in loving the distance between them which makes it possible for each to see the other whole against a wide sky.

The Friendship Factor

4

Marriage as Sacrament
Human Love as a Sign

> For what can be known about God is plain to them, because God has shown it to them. Ever since the creation of the world his eternal power and divine nature, invisible though they are, have been understood and seen through the things he has made.
>
> —ROMANS 1:19–20

Just before Mass one Sunday, a man pushed his wife's wheelchair up the aisle and settled down in the pew in front of us. He unbuttoned her coat, opened up her collar, and pulled out a soft white bib, which he carefully positioned beneath her chin. She sat motionless in her chair in a bright red leather jacket, the effects of a stroke evident—head dropped slightly forward, eyes open and attentive. The man was intent on praying the Mass, but he often instinctively reached over now and then to touch his wife's hand or catch a drool or sniffle with the white bib. He kissed her on the forehead at the kiss of peace. When he returned from communion he ever-so-carefully placed a small piece of the host on her tongue, watching to make sure she swallowed it.

I was deeply touched by the entire loving connection between this couple. There we were, at the sacramental celebration of Christ's unconditional and self-sacrificing love in the Eucharist. And sitting in front of me was a powerful human example of that same love manifested in the sacrament of marriage

When couples answer the call to love unconditionally in the vocation of marriage, their relationship becomes a sign of God's love in the world. Thus, the church views marriage as a sacrament.

According to the Catechism of the Catholic Church, sacraments are "efficacious signs of grace, instituted by Christ and entrusted to the Church, by which divine life is dispensed to us" (1131). The key word in this sentence is *efficacious*. This means "producing or capable of producing a desired effect." A sacrament is a sign—something (or in the case of marriage, someone) that symbolizes and points to another reality. But it is an *efficacious* sign; that is, it is a sign that *achieves* the reality. The care-giving husband was not only a sign for me of unconditional love but he was also bringing that love into the world for his wife in the pew in front of me. The water of baptism is a sign of new life in Christ, but it also confers that new life on the person being baptized. Similarly, the union of man and woman in marriage is a sign of God's love for human beings. But it also conveys this love to us. In other words, marriage shows that God loves us, but it is also a means through which God loves us.

Think for a moment about what that means in your daily life. What would it look like if you loved as God loves when the car was out of gas, or you bounced a check or forgot a birthday? How does God love in the real world of married life?

The Scriptures give us a clear picture of how one might love as God loves. "The LORD is gracious and merciful, slow to anger and abounding in steadfast love," says the psalmist. God's love is life-giving. It is merciful and forgives seventy times seven. God's love is sacrificial and self-emptying. It is compassionate, faithful, healing, and ready to feed and nourish wherever there is hunger. God's love is directed with special compassion on the poor and outcast. If you read the Gospels, the life of Jesus will give you a very concrete view of how God loves.

A remarkable Old Testament story about a marriage adds further depth to our understanding of God's love for us. This is the story of Hosea, who was married to the harlot, Gomer. She was repeatedly unfaithful to Hosea, but Hosea always took her back, even though he had every right to cast her out of his home. When Gomer strayed, Hosea waited patiently for her return. Hosea's faithfulness reflects God's love for his people. The people of Israel were chronically unfaithful to their covenant with God; they broke God's laws and repeatedly worshipped other gods. Yahweh always took them back in spite of their offenses.

Hosea's love for Gomer is a prophetic symbol of Yahweh's love for Israel and of Jesus' relationship with the church. It points toward a fuller, deeper, and richer reality to come. This symbol says to us that "despite appearances, something greater is going on here." This is an especially appropriate message about marriage because no marriage ever measures up to the fullness of the ideal. We can only approach the ideal. We taste the profound connection between married love and Christ's love over time as we grow in our commitment and learn to care for one another. We didn't "receive" the sacrament of marriage on our wedding day, as though it were some magic bullet that transformed us into loving signs. We grow into a sacramental union to the extent that we cooperate with the grace given to us.

Not every marriage reflects the love and steadfast fidelity of God. To experience marriage as a sacrament presupposes some degree of love between spouses and some level of relationship with Christ. The grace of the sacrament of marriage builds on the existing potential for love and faithfulness, which the spouses bring to their "I do." Becoming married and becoming a sacrament—both are lifelong processes.

Name a couple who have been a sign for you of God's love and fidelity. What qualities of God's love did you see in them?

What thoughts and feelings do you have as you reflect on yourself as a sacramental sign?

Most Catholics are familiar with the idea of sacraments, but it's difficult to think "sacramentally." We are accustomed to viewing life pragmatically; what you see is what you get. By contrast, the sacramental lens shows us that the everyday things of this world are windows into another world. They show us the mysteries of God.

One of those windows is human love and friendship. True friendship is something of a miracle. The notion of friendship in the Christian spiritual tradition connotes an attraction to something good in another. Friends are those who see good in us and desire good for us. They are concerned with our welfare. We cherish the people who know us and with whom we can share anything. Our friends put flesh on God for us.

One of the worst weeks of my life happened during the time when my mother was dying. She had lost her battle with cancer, and was in the hospital gradually slipping away. I was absorbed in this crisis and had no time or emotional resources for anything else. The day of my son's ninth birthday was approaching; I had to tell him that we couldn't have a party until sometime later, after grandma died and the funeral was over. Of course he was disappointed. I told a good friend of mine how much it broke my heart to let him down this way.

Two days later, I came home from the hospital to find a full-blown birthday party in progress. My son was in the backyard playing games with his friends. The house was decorated for a party, with ice cream and cake in abundance. My friend had planned the whole thing.

I was surprised and grateful. This good friend cared about me; through what she did, I understood that God cared about me too. My friend's act of generosity during that terrible week gave me a glimpse of God that words cannot adequately describe. I've read books by saints and mystics that attempt to describe their intense personal experience of God's presence. Words fail them. They are trying to describe the indescribable. Something similar happened to me that day. My friend's generosity was a sacramental sign that gave me an intense experience of God.

The theologian Bernard Cooke goes so far as to say that human friendship—personal love—is the basic sacrament of God's presence. This sacrament (with a small "s") is "a special avenue of insight into the reality of God," he writes. The Gospels show clearly that God's presence in the world unfolds in the context of loving human relationships. Jesus didn't speak abstractly about love and the coming of God's kingdom. He showed this love in practical ways by healing Peter's mother-in-law, changing water into wine at a wedding feast, and raising Lazarus from the dead before the eyes of his grieving family. The night before he died, he gave himself in the Eucharist at a ritual meal shared with his most intimate friends.

For most people, the love of another human being is the most tangible sign of the existence of a loving God. Married life gives us the opportunity to experience this kind of friendship. We manifest God's love through small things: a compliment, a gentle touch, making a cup of tea. We show love through the big things too: repeatedly forgiving each other, and sticking together through financial stress, illness, and family tragedies.

On your wedding day, in the sacramental rite that you celebrated, you were the symbols of the sacrament. Like the bread and wine in the sacrament of Eucharist, you will be transformed by the Holy Spirit in your efforts at lifelong friendship. Each of you is called to be a sacrament to the other. That's a large order! Few, if any, couples achieve this level of friendship on a daily basis, but your efforts at faithfulness and love proclaim, make present, and celebrate the reality of God's love in the world!

In what ways has your spouse been a best friend to you?

What does that friendship reveal to you about God's love?

A Marriage for Others

Jason and Patty have three children of their own and are raising a fourth child whose parents died in a fire several years ago. Like most families, they try to attend most of their kids' sports events and struggle to juggle work schedules with quality time together. On her way home from a part-time job at the hospital, Patty stops to check on her aging mother-in-law who lives alone and needs some help in taking medications and getting around. She often brings her eleven-year-old son with her to do yard work or help grandma with chores.

They are like most families trying to make ends meet and to impose some order on their hectic lives. Jason volunteers several times a year in building a Habitat for Humanity home in the city where they live, and he always takes one or another of the older children with him. Their neighbors and friends know that if they are ever in a pinch, they can depend on Jason and Patty to listen or lend a hand or loan out a child for babysitting.

Marriage is the most intimate of relationships, but it is also a public institution. Like all the sacraments, marriage conveys God's love to the larger community as well as to the individuals involved. It's easy to lose sight of this social dimension of marriage.

Viewed with the lens of faith, Jason and Patty are a sign for others. In a small way, they are not only showing their friends and family how God loves, they are also bringing God's love into the world in very practical ways. What is God like? We know God is love; God is compassionate and generous. Above all, God is faithful. In their everyday lives, faithful spouses proclaim to society that we can always count on God.

In the Christian tradition we call the home that Jason and Patty have created a "domestic church," the basic unit of the larger church.

Children first learn about God's love from their family. But the family is also a basic unit of society; marriage and family life provide a school of social responsibility. Though most of our homes don't reflect the order and organization of a school, the home is still the place where a child first learns—or doesn't learn—how to be a responsible citizen. By their example couples teach children the difference between right and wrong. Kids learn respect for others and for their property and for the law. They learn honesty, a sense of service, and responsibility for the common good (or not). Society depends on the home to do this basic education of its members.

The social impact of your marriage will change over time. As you establish and maintain a household, you will naturally be drawn by your friends or children into social situations and connections that will require your time and talents. You are asked to volunteer for projects, coach teams, and participate in parish and community organizations. You will serve the community in different ways across the years and have opportunities to use your gifts and energy for others. You marriage will be like a lighthouse. You will witness your values in subtle ways: how you use your money, your time, and your talents at home and in the community. The light of your love will shine through in your hospitality to others, your coaching or volunteering in politics or parish life. Some days the light shines brightly, and at times it's dimmer, but it's always visible. It's a sign that's always on.

Your light is seen by others around you but is most visible to your children. Children are always absorbing your attitudes, values, and habits. From your example, they are learning how to deal with conflict, develop mutual respect, express affection, and develop trust in the opposite sex. You are a walking, talking text about how to love and forgive. Research by the sociologist Judith Siegel shows conclusively that what children observe in their parents' marriage is the blueprint for their own relationships. For the most part, this is a hidden influence. Children are largely unaware of how their parents' love guided them, at least until they become adults themselves, and often not even then. Parents, too, are often blind to this influence. This is all the more reason for spouses to consistently practice the disciplines of marital love. You never know who's watching, and what they're learning from you.

Name something positive and something negative that your children may be learning (or will learn) from your marriage.

As you reflect on your activities in the community, where are opportunities for you to be a sign to others of God's love and fidelity?

Couple Charisms

The impact your marriage has on others will be uniquely your own because it is fed and energized by your specific talents and gifts. The word the New Testament uses for these gifts is *charism*. The Holy Spirit gives us charisms for the sake of others, "to equip the saints for the work of ministry, for building up the body of Christ," as Paul writes (Ephesians 4:12). I believe that marriages have unique gifts too. I call them "couple charisms."

A couple I know has a ministry of hospitality; they serve brunch on most Sundays after Mass to welcome new people into the parish. Another couple, widely experienced in the world of work, help their nieces and nephews and other young people write effective resumes and cover letters so they can get good jobs. Another couple we know has made a special commitment to serving mentally impaired people in their community; they volunteer at halfway houses and lobby the city and county for more funding for services. The life of one couple we know well has been shaped by the needs of their severely disabled son. They have made great sacrifices for him; he is constantly with them. All these couples are powerful beacons of love, touching many lives.

Often one partner in a marriage will take the lead in a particular service and the other spouse will play a supportive role. Our friends Chad and Donna are one example. Chad coaches football, basketball, and track at a Catholic high school. His teams are successful, but Chad's special talent is mentoring teenage boys who are learning to become men. He has made an extraordinary impact on the lives of countless men over twenty years of coaching. Chad couldn't do this work without Donna's active and generous support. She makes it possible for him to live the busy schedule that his work requires. Chad and Donna view this work as their joint ministry as a couple, even though few people are aware of the indispensable role Donna plays.

These are some of the ways your marriage takes on a deeper richness and significance when viewed through the lens of sacrament. Your acts of love and faithfulness to each other in good times and bad become signs of God's love and fidelity. This kind of sign is powerful; it is an *efficacious* sign that actually brings about the love and fidelity it symbolizes. God is directly, immediately present in your life through the love and care and service of your spouse. God is also present in the world through your marriage. When you serve others through your individual or couple charisms, God is in fact serving them through your life.

Make a list of the gifts/talents/positive traits that your spouse possesses.

Which do you especially value and which are valued by others?

How do you support and empower each other's gifts for the good of the home and community?

If you truly see your relationship as a light for others, what effect will that have on the way you approach your life together?

From the Catechism

1617 The entire Christian life bears the mark of the spousal love of Christ and the Church. Already Baptism, the entry into the People of God, is a nuptial mystery; it is so to speak the nuptial bath which precedes the wedding feast, the Eucharist. Christian marriage in its turn becomes an efficacious sign, the sacrament of the covenant of Christ and the Church. Since it signifies and communicates grace, marriage between baptized persons is a true sacrament of the New Covenant.

5

Marriage as Covenant
For Better, for Worse, with God

Scott and Tina were college sweethearts. They married right after graduation and had their first child before their first anniversary. Two other children followed. Tina stayed home with the children while Scott moved ahead in his career in the computer industry. But then things changed. Scott lost two jobs, and settled for lower-paying, less-satisfying work. Then his intermittent problem with alcohol became a full-blown crisis. Scott was unemployed for several years. Tina returned to work, had a miscarriage, all the while encouraging Scott to seek help. Eventually he entered treatment and began recovery that has continued.

Life is much better today for Tina and Scott. They have been through hard times, terrible times. But they told me a beautiful thing: through their twenty-two years of marriage, neither doubted the love of the other. They always believed they were loved even when problems kept them from showing it. They didn't always feel the other's love but they never lost sight of their promise and their desire to love each other until death.

In the nuptial blessing at the wedding Mass, the presider says that God "made the union of husband and wife an image of the covenant between you and your people." Covenant love is steadfast love—it is love that endures. Scott and Tina's marriage vividly illustrates the depth and strength of covenant love. The lens of faith reveals the profound and intimate connection between human commitment and God's steadfast love for humanity.

Your marriage covenant is rooted in your baptism. In order to contract for a civil marriage you need a birth certificate, but for a Catholic marriage you need proof of baptism and confirmation. In baptism you were united with Christ and incorporated into his church. When you join with your spouse in marriage, you make a covenant together that reflects the deep commitment of love and fidelity between Christ and the church. Covenant is the third lens through which we will look at marriage. With vocation and sacrament, it further reveals the thread of God's presence woven through the fabric of your life together.

In the eyes of the state, the promises you exchanged on your wedding day constitute a *contract*. Your marriage, like all marriages, is a legally binding agreement with rights and privileges that are spelled out in civil law. If one party to a contract violates its terms, the contract becomes null and void. A contract can also be ended by mutual agreement.

A covenant is different from a contract in that a covenant requires each partner to make a radical, permanent commitment to the other. The one making the covenant is bound by its terms even if the other party is unfaithful to them. Like most couples, Scott and Tina probably had no idea what their vows really meant until they faced the daily demands of fidelity.

Covenant is an ancient word that refers to God's relationship with his people. God made the original covenant with the people of Israel; he took the initiative, saying, "I will place my dwelling in your midst, and I shall not abhor you. And I will walk among you, and will be your God, and you shall be my people" (Leviticus 26:11–12). The people of Israel did not hold up their end of the covenant; they repeatedly violated God's law, worshipped other gods, and ignored his direction. Nevertheless, God continued to love and care for his people.

Eventually, God made a new covenant through the coming of Jesus, and thereby extended covenant love to the entire human race.

The promises made on your wedding day are covenant promises. They are not easy to fulfill. Those promises are a way of participating in the promise God makes to us. Because God's grace abides in the sacrament of matrimony, grace makes covenant promising possible. God's unconditional love is the source of marital love, the well from which you and your partner can draw throughout your married life, "for richer or poorer, in good times and in bad, in sickness and in health, till death."

When We Say No to Say Yes

Tina had doubts many times in the dark days of her marriage. She would look at other men and wonder whether she had made the wrong choice in marrying Scott. Scott had his despairing moments too. When he was unemployed and struggling with alcohol, he would wonder whether he should just walk away from his family. But neither of them acted on these thoughts; they persevered.

In addition to being unending, covenant love is exclusive. Covenant love is boundless and unconditional, but it is focused.

Israel had to say no to many things in order to say yes to their covenant to Yahweh. The people had to forsake the gods and goddesses that they believed provided good crops, the birth of children, and protection from their enemies. They had to submit to a Law that governed the activities of daily life in some detail. They shouldered the special responsibilities that came with being God's people.

The same is true in the marriage covenant. Husband and wife say no to many things in order to say yes to each other. They "forsake all others." By definition, marriage is exclusive, husband and wife renouncing all other men and women when they say "I do." They also forsake many of their preferences, ideas, and attitudes for the sake of their common life. The marriage might require one or both of the partners to leave a job they love and embark on a new career. It might mean settling in a new place, far away from family and friends. The marriage will certainly require the partners to say no to some of their desires: the new pickup truck, the remodeled kitchen, the vacation cruise, the season football tickets. It will mean painful compromise concerning favorite habits and the relinquishing of some cherished ideas about the way things should be.

Christians call this process "dying to self." It is one of the essential spiritual disciplines of every vocational path. Dying to self is a way to imitate Jesus in the details of our lives, and it is a way to participate in his dying and rising. This is a holy process. At our baptism, we were plunged (the literal meaning of the word from which *baptism* is derived) into the death and resurrection of Jesus. That rite at the baptismal font didn't stop there but continues throughout life. Dying to self is a spiritual task and is essential to covenant living. It is possible only through the power of the Holy Spirit, also given to us at baptism and confirmation. Jesus said that the Father will send the Spirit "in my name, will teach you everything, and remind you of all that I have said to you" (John 14:26). We are assured of this divine help in the daily dyings required by covenant love.

Consider a time recently when you have said no to something or some opportunity for the sake of your spouse or your marriage. In what way did this no become a yes to your spouse and a benefit to your marriage? What did you think/feel about your choice?

How would your attitude toward the no be changed if you saw that decision as a way of following through on your covenant promise to your spouse?

How Covenant
Changes the Individual

Scott looks back sadly on the dark days when he was unemployed, struggling with alcoholism, and was generally AWOL in his marriage and home. The bright spot for him was Tina's love during those times. Her fidelity gave him a powerful experience of God's love for him; he eventually responded to this love and overcame his addiction. Tina's love transformed Scott. He didn't see it then, but he can see it now.

A covenant changes the people who are parties to it. When I ask couples how they have been changed by their experience of marriage, they humorously point to their waistlines. But they all acknowledge that their covenant promise at the altar started a process of personal transformation. They flailed away in their efforts to be faithful, but they nevertheless have become more patient, humble, and other-centered. It's hard for them to explain how this happens. With differing degrees of humility they talk about how God helped them in certain situations. I think that's another way of saying that the grace of the sacrament is at work in its mysterious way when we love selflessly.

The great example of covenant transformation in the Bible is Yahweh's covenant with Israel. The covenant changed everything for the Hebrew people. Before the covenant they were a demoralized, discontented, ragtag crowd of former slaves wandering in the desert. The covenant relationship with God transformed them, giving them an identity, a purpose, a way of life, a mission, and a land of their own. Similarly, the marriage covenant forms the partners in new and surprising ways.

They see themselves differently—a man becomes "a husband" and a woman becomes "a wife." They set about building something that never existed before: a new family, a common enterprise, an "us." With the arrival of children, new responsibilities appear. As the partners in marriage swim in this process of continual change, they are transformed, sometimes by choice, other times by necessity. They grow stronger in some areas and lose ground in others. In looking back on their lives together, couples agree that times of stress and anxiety are often the most transformative.

Recent research suggests that changing your attitudes and habits for the sake of another person is the psychologically healthy thing to do. John Gottman, a noted marriage therapist and researcher, conducted a fifteen-year study of married couples, looking for the qualities that are associated with long-lasting and satisfying marriages. He found that spouses' willingness to yield to the other person is a major predictor of marital success. We are re-formed when we yield to another person out of love. Whether it's deciding how strong to make the coffee or how much money to put in the IRA, covenant love calls us to defer to one another out of love for Christ.

Recall some of the changes that occurred in you since you were married.

- What has inspired or caused these changes?
- Turn to your spouse and name one positive change you see in yourself.

- Name a positive change in your spouse and why you appreciate it.

How would your attitude toward these changes be different if you saw them as God's way of transforming you through the covenant of love you made with your spouse?

Why Change Is Slow and Not Always Steady

Above all, trust in the slow work of God. We are quite naturally impatient in everything to reach the end without delay. We should like to skip the intermediate stages. We are impatient of being on the way to something unknown, something new.

And yet it is in the law of all progress that it is made by passing through some stages of instability . . . and that may take a very long time.

And so it is with you. Your ideas mature gradually . . . let them grow, let them shape themselves without undue haste. Don't try to "force" them on, as though you could be today what time [that is to say, grace and circumstances acting on your own good will] will make you tomorrow.

Only God could say what this new spirit, gradually forming within you, will be. Believe that God's hand is leading you surely through the obscurity and the becoming, and accept the anxiety of feeling yourself in suspense and incomplete.

— Pierre Teilhard de Chardin

After twenty-two years of marriage, Scott and Tina look back on a relationship that has changed many times. They were college sweethearts, and the first years of their marriage were colored by a carefree romantic spirit. The marriage changed with the responsibilities of parenthood. Then it changed drastically when hard times came and Tina carried the load. It changed again when Scott faced his problems and began to recover. In a sense they lived several marriages.

Not only does a covenant marriage change the two partners, but it changes the relationship as well. Covenant relationships are developmental. A look at God's covenant with us helps us see how our covenant changes over time.

God expressed his covenant love for his people in very different ways as their relationship progressed. At the beginning, he dramatically delivered them from slavery in Egypt and fed them in the desert. As the people settled the Promised Land, God gave them a way of life and the institutions of a people. Later he gave them a temple for worship and a king to lead them. When the people strayed, God expressed his love through the chastisement of the prophets. Finally, God gave himself—the covenant with Israel was transformed into the New Covenant of Jesus Christ, who brought God to live with his people forever.

These great changes in the covenant were perceived most clearly in retrospect. Israel understood that they had become a people when they looked back on the mighty things God had done for them. Ironically, they saw what God had done for them after they had lost so much. The story of the covenant was written by the Jews after they had been driven away from the Promised Land and into exile. The bitter experience of ruin and defeat, and distance from their former life, gave them the perspective necessary to understand the glory of God's love for them.

The same thing is often true in marriage. We see what we have become when we look back. Scott and Tina may not have been able to name their experience of grace while they were living it, but they had a basic confidence in God during their dark times. They understood how well God had cared for them only later, when they reflected on their experience.

We see the same covenant as a process of transformation over time in the New Testament. The Gospels and the Acts of the Apostles show the transformation of the relationship between Jesus and his disciples. The disciples continually misunderstood his teaching and failed to grasp his mission. They saw him as a messianic king who would restore Israel's political glory. Only with Jesus' death and resurrection did his friends begin to comprehend his spiritual mission; then, finally, they saw that he would be a spiritual partner to them. One of the most touching stories in the New Testament is the account of Jesus' encounter with two disciples on the road to Emmaus. The story teaches that Jesus is present to us in the Eucharist, and that the story of our relationship with him becomes clearer as we look back on what he has done.

Similarly, our eyes are opened to the mysteries of marriage only over time and usually in retrospect. We literally don't know what we are getting ourselves into when we exchange vows at the altar. You don't "get married" on your wedding day—you *begin* to be married that day. In all the years that follow you learn what it means to be married. You change, your spouse changes, circumstances change, and you face new challenges and take advantage of new opportunities. You express love in different ways, and your marriage is different from one season to the next.

I can see this process of change in my own marriage. In our early years together I was the breadwinner for the family while my husband completed graduate studies. I worked, he stayed home and studied. After our first child was born, I stayed home to care full-time for our baby, and my husband began a demanding career. It took us several years to renegotiate our relationship and to find ways of keeping house, caring for children, and addressing my needs for intellectual stimulation and social connections. When I later returned to work, another renegotiation was necessary. Our roles changed, as did our expectations of each other. As we faced job changes, children leaving home, and care of our aging parents, our relationship and roles—and even the depth of our commitment—changed again. The first renegotiated marriage was the hardest; after that, the next ones came easier because we knew we could be flexible and hang in there for periods of transition and eventually arrive at a new "us" that was satisfying and challenging at the same time.

Discuss with your spouse the changes in your marriage relationship:

- Talk about one change in the relationship that happened as a result of your choices (career change, going back to school, having another child).
- Talk about one change that happened because circumstances changed (illness, job loss, accident).

As you look back at the process of change within and among you, how did you experience God's presence in that process?

Covenant Love: More Than a Feeling

The covenant love that forms and shapes us in marriage is something far deeper and richer than the romantic notion of love that permeates the media. The popular meaning of love conveys powerful, perhaps overwhelming, romantic feelings, especially feelings of sensual passion. Passion and romance are important parts of marriage, but they are only part; covenant love involves much more. There's a developmental process whereby the experience of marital love grows deeper, more complex, and more satisfying. In most marriages, the partners will express love to each other in different ways as the years go by.

My description of the dimensions of married love draws on the work of Drs. Les and Leslie Parrott. In their book, *Saving Your Marriage Before It Starts*, they describe the dimensions of married love as romance, intimacy, and commitment. These might be seen as aspects of covenant love, and they represent an ever-deepening relationship.

Romance

Spouses today expect to find each other physically attractive and emotionally attuned. Feelings of affection and the promise of sexual satisfaction are key considerations for marriage today, but this was not always the case. For most of human history, marriages were ruled by economic and social considerations—and this is still the case in some cultures. The feelings of the prospective husband and wife were given scant consideration.

In most marriages in the United States, feelings are paramount. Romance burns brightly, especially in the first years of marriage, but this changes. For many couples the wife is the first to notice the change in levels of romance while husbands notice a downturn in frequency of sex. Spouses discover their differences, including differences in temperament and personality. Some people are naturally quite affectionate and emotionally expressive, while others are not—the two types often wind up married to each other. The arrival of children drastically affects romance in marriage. The stresses of parenting and the pressures of work and homemaking eat up time and erode emotional energy. After about five years of marriage, many couples find themselves feeling wistful when they hear romantic songs and watch romantic movies. Where did the romance go? It's no accident that most of the passionate lovemaking depicted in movies and TV shows takes place between people who are not married; we are not accustomed to thinking of the typical marriage as being full of romantic passion.

Romantic love is a function of the heart. It is an important part of marriage, but it becomes harder to sustain as the years go by. Couples have to work at romance in the long-term. Married couples looking for renewal in their relationship are often advised to restore to their lives the expressions of romance and affection that once came naturally. Renewing old and finding new expressions of romance and affection increases emotional closeness and deepens couple unity. This is part of the work of the vocation of marriage to "become one." It's wise to treat romance like a bank account—make frequent emotional deposits that you can draw on later when things get tough. Covenant love in marriage includes the romantic dimension of desiring the beloved and savoring the presence of each other.

In what ways are your experiences of romance different now from your first years of marriage? What experiences/ actions promote feelings of closeness and unity for you now?

What one thing could you or your spouse do to foster romance in your marriage—to "make a deposit in your emotional bank account"? (Write down your answers separately and share the answers with your spouse.)

Intimacy

As the marriage grows, husband and wife truly get to know each other. If they are communicating well, they become familiar with each other's likes and dislikes, fears and joys, hopes and dreams. They share their past lives with each other in detail, and they forge a common vision for the future. They become familiar with each other's annoying habits and endearing traits. This is the experience of marital intimacy—the experience of being truly known and loved by another person. Intimacy is the fruit of gathering a thorough knowledge of each other over time.

Couples don't gain this knowledge automatically, because intimacy deepens with effort. The psychologist John Gottman refers to "emotionally intelligent" couples. These are the spouses who pay close attention to each other's cares and concerns on a daily basis. They make a consistent effort to know about each other's work, friends, ideas, hobbies, and feelings. Gottman found that emotionally intelligent couples tend to be more satisfied with their marriages than couples who do not work intentionally at achieving intimacy.

This deep knowledge and attentiveness to each other is part of "belonging" to each other. When we say "I take you to be my husband/wife" we do not mean "take possession" but "take you" as a beloved partner on life's journey. This experience gives couples a glimpse of God's posture toward us.

While romance is a function of the heart, intimacy is a function of the mind. It comes to a large degree from knowledge about your spouse's life. You don't gain this knowledge from conversations that consist of exchanges of information about practical matters. Intimacy in a covenanted love relationship is the fruit of active listening and eager mutual sharing. Romantic feelings can perhaps make the work of intimacy a bit easier, but intimacy encompasses much more. In fact, intimacy heightens romance. Passion deepens when lovers know the dark as well as the light, and still accept each other unconditionally.

In what ways could you foster listening and conversation that is honest mutual sharing? Consider these options:

- a weekly date night
- reading or listening to a book on communication skills
- addressing a problem or issue that is an obstacle to communication toward intimacy

An exercise for deeper conversation: Complete the following statements separately, then share answers.

One thing I would like to make more time for in my day is
_____

One of my greatest fears is _____

A person who is bugging me the most right now is
_____

One or two greatest aspirations/hopes I have are
_____

Commitment

A covenant marriage is characterized by steadfast fidelity; the partners are committed to each other. Their marriage is a choice—they chose each other on their wedding day, and they continue to choose each other every day. Some days they're married to the man or woman of their dreams, and some days they're married to the family and home they've created together. Some days they're married to the marriage. Some days, the decision to be married is a tough one, when circumstances are hard and romance and intimacy are at a low ebb. In these times, commitment, an essential dimension of covenant love, carries couples through.

Renowned marriage researcher Scott Stanley in his book, *The Heart of Commitment*, says that commitment comes in two forms: dedication and constraint. Dedication, he says, is "an internal state of devotion to a person or object." Dedication sets your course; it's the inner conviction that keeps you steadily pursuing a goal. Constraints are the limits and the costs; they remind you that there's a price to be paid if you get off the path or step over the limits. Dedication draws you forward, while constraint pushes you from behind.

Dedication and constraint both play a role in the marriage. You might willingly make the personal sacrifices necessary in marriage from the highest spiritual motives and purest devotion to your spouse. But you are also mindful that there's a price to be paid if you don't make these sacrifices: your common life will suffer, your children will suffer, and ultimately the marriage itself could be in danger. A desire to avoid divorce is a major constraint that keeps many couples committed to their marriages when they may not want to be.

For most couples the commitment to covenant marriage is composed of both dedication and constraint. Together they form a bond of steadfast love that makes covenant living possible. In his covenant relationship with the Israelites, Yahweh gave the Law—which was a constraint—as a means of keeping the people on course with the covenant.

Likewise, marriage is a pledge of love and fidelity that you and your spouse make to each other with God as the Source of that love. This relationship transforms husband and wife as they grow in commitment to each other, sometimes through dedication and sometimes because of constraints.

The lens of covenant reveals great richness and beauty in your marriage. It shows us the connection between our daily efforts to be faithful and the steadfast love of God, who is always present with us. Though the promises we made at the altar are sealed by God's promise of unconditional love for us, we cannot afford to adopt a "let God do it" stance. Growing in romance, intimacy, and commitment takes action on our part—a fact upheld by our own experience and by scientific research.

Complete the sentence: I am committed to my spouse and our marriage because . . . (list all the reasons you can think of)

Which reasons reflect dedication commitment and which reflect constraint commitment? Is one factor stronger than another?

How can you as a couple deepen your dedication to each other?

From the Catechism

1646 By its very nature conjugal love requires the inviolable fidelity of the spouses. This is the consequence of the gift of themselves which they make to each other. Love seeks to be definitive; it cannot be an arrangement "until further notice." The "intimate union of marriage, as a mutual giving of two persons, and the good of the children, demand total fidelity from the spouses and require an unbreakable union between them."

6

Couple Spirituality
The Mystery in the Mundane

A husband works two jobs to pay for the expensive formula his new baby requires. A wife comforts her grieving husband whose father has died. A couple savors a beautiful sunset together. Husband and wife make love. Parents stand in awe at the birth of a new child. Spouses pray together each morning before leaving for work. A couple spends the weekend helping a neighbor move. A spouse changes jobs so that his partner can continue graduate studies in another city.

These are all examples of sacramental love at work. All of them are expressions of couple spirituality. They illustrate what it means for married persons to encounter God in the ordinary experiences of daily life.

Couple spirituality rests on the foundation of the theology of marriage that has been presented in the first part of this book. We've looked at marriage as a vocation—a way of life that will draw you into a closer relationship with God. It is also a sacrament that makes you and your spouse a sign of God's love to each other and to the world. Finally, marriage is a covenant relationship in which God's steadfast fidelity and love are always at work.

These theological dimensions of marriage are lenses that allow you to see your marriage in a new light. They bring out shades and tones and details that would otherwise be hidden. Your marriage is not simply a practical arrangement or a daily round of chores, appointments, and responsibilities, though it may seem that way on most days. It's a spiritual adventure bringing you, your spouse, and God into a dynamic and life-giving partnership, a relationship that is a "holy mystery."

A New Recognition
of Couple Spirituality

Christian couples have walked the path of holiness for centuries, but "couple spirituality" has only recently been emphasized in Catholic thinking. The classic spiritualities of the Catholic tradition mainly reflect the lives of celibate men and women. Benedictine spirituality, one of the most ancient, was developed in monastic communities. It emphasizes hospitality, praying the liturgy of the hours, and achieving a balance between work and prayer in daily life. Franciscan spirituality emphasizes reverence for creation and a spirit of poverty. Ignatian spirituality stresses the importance of uniting oneself with God's work in the world.

These spiritualities have much to offer couples. They incorporate great wisdom about our relationship with God, and they include disciplines, prayers, and exercises that nourish that relationship. But the traditional spiritualities have some limitations. They emerged from the lives of groups of celibate people engaged in strenuous apostolic work: education, care of the sick, social justice, or round-the-clock prayer in convents and monasteries. Marriage and family life were not part of the daily experience of these priests, monks, and vowed religious. An attitude took hold that a religious vocation was a higher calling than the married life, and that people who wanted to truly experience intimacy with God had to be free of the distractions of marriage and family.

This, of course, is not so. In recent years, Catholic teachers and pastors have come to a deeper appreciation of the fact that intimacy with God is available to everyone in every walk of life. There is only one spirituality: the call to live as a follower of Christ. We can live out this call in various ways. For married people, intimacy with God comes precisely through relationships with family.

Married people have always known this, but they haven't always spoken or written about it. For most of Catholic history, the vast majority of married people were illiterate. Literate clergy and religious could write about their experience of God, but married people, by and large, could not. The spread of literacy and education in the past two centuries has given married people the tools to articulate their experiences of God. The Second Vatican Council gave them the encouragement to do this; the council emphasized the dignity of the married vocation and the vocation of the laity. It spoke of the family as the domestic church. In the years since the council, married couples have been encouraged to reflect on their unique path to holiness, a path that leads through the kitchen, the bedroom, and the backyard.

Helping couples reflect on their spiritual experiences is a major goal of this book. We are still learning how to talk about couple spirituality, which is a "grass roots" spirituality—a path to God that requires reflection on our experience in light of faith.

What images, activities, and words come to mind when you hear the term "couple spirituality"? Write down the answers separately.

Discuss the answers with your spouse. Which images do you find most appealing? Least appealing? Why?

The Need for Religious Practices in Marriage

An important aspect of couple spirituality is participation in religious practices. For instance, prayer is the foundation of the spiritual life—this is true for the vocation of marriage as well as ordained life or single life. Prayer, whether by an individual or a couple, is an indispensable source of strength and growth. Praying together opens pathways to deeper communion between husband and wife, and prayer is the dialogue of the covenant between spouses and God. Other religious practices strengthen and deepen married life as well: worshipping with a believing community; receiving the sacraments together; observing religious rituals and traditions; participating in faith sharing groups; and serving others, especially the poor and marginalized. Religious practices fuel the fire of married spirituality.

But couple spirituality includes much more than religious practices. In fact, the unique aspects of marital spirituality have to do with the intricate web of relationships between spouses and those who enter the circle of their love. God works in the day-to-day circumstances of married life, and so the richness of couple spirituality lies not only in prayer and religious practice but also in discerning the presence of God in the ways you spend your money, raise your children, and resolve your conflicts.

The phrase *marriage is a holy mystery* from the wedding liturgy applies here. We know that God is present in our world (including the world of marriage and family), but we can't fully understand how this is so. God created the world and all that's in it and pronounced it good. In the person of Jesus, God entered the world in the most intimate fashion, an astounding fact so enormous in its implications that it's impossible to grasp them all. It's difficult to even speak and write about them. St. Thomas Aquinas reminded us that all human language about God is a metaphor, an approximation of something that cannot be described.

When it comes to seeing the hand of God at work in our married lives, we see through a glass darkly. We can catch a glimpse of the divine in a comforting embrace or the beauty of a sleeping child. Our understanding is always imperfect, and it usually lags behind the experience.

Rick and JoAnn engaged in a long struggle to help their daughter Lisa cope with social and academic problems at school. The problems were potentially serious, and so Rick and JoAnn devoted many hours to patient work, helping their daughter with schoolwork. They prayed for her, and they worked with teachers and counselors. Rick changed jobs, partly to spend more time at home. JoAnn changed her schedule so she could be with Lisa in the late afternoons. Rick and JoAnn learned better ways to communicate with Lisa and with each other. Their efforts paid off; after a year or so, Lisa's grades improved and she had an easier time making friends.

Initially, Rick and JoAnn did not perceive this struggle as a spiritual experience. To them, it was work—slow, frustrating, and sometimes heartbreaking. In retrospect, they were able to see that God was present in their efforts to help their daughter. God entered their lives through this difficult struggle. Rick and JoAnn had faith that God was caring for Lisa, in large part through their own care for her and through the help and support of others. They learned how to find hope in the midst of frustration and disappointment. They grew in their love for each other by sharing the experience of helping their daughter through a difficult time in her life. The year-long crisis deepened their spiritual lives in faith, hope, and love.

Marital spirituality is like that. Though we sometimes do things intentionally to find God's presence, more often we recognize God's presence in retrospect. The great spiritual truth about marriage is that God is present in the very relationship between persons; in the love and forgiveness, in the patience and dedication, even in the unresolved anger and hurt. The mystery lies in the way the spiritual truths coexist with, and emerge from, the most mundane circumstances.

Name some religious practices that have enriched your individual relationship with God. (Religious practices include devotions, rituals, traditions, prayer practices, worship, etc.)

If you are in an interfaith marriage, what are some common practices that you share?

What religious practices have helped build a strong bond between you? Name two or three, and discuss what they have done for your marriage.

In addition to these religious practices, share with your spouse a moment when you witnessed God's presence in your experience of marriage.

The Practice of Recognizing God's Presence

Recognizing God's presence isn't like taking God's picture at some peak moment in time and admiring it in a frame on your desk. It's a lifelong process of seeing more clearly and deeply, and of cleaning off the lens and slowing down in order to gaze more intently.

Sometimes God's presence is palpable. I remember being rolled down a hospital hallway on the way to surgery, full of fear. My husband walked alongside holding my hand. When we reached the doors of the white-tiled operating room, he kissed me. At that moment a profound peace came over me; I felt as if God's peace had entered the hallway to calm me.

Most people can point to moments like these when God seems very near. Yet these instances, when a black and yellow "God at Work" sign loudly announces his presence, are actually quite rare. More often, God's presence is harder to discern. For this we can turn to Catholic tradition for help. Church teachings and the Scriptures give us a clearer look at how divine presence can be understood.

One of the most important of these teachings is the doctrine of the Trinity, the teaching that God exists as three divine persons sharing in one divine nature. Chances are you don't think about the Trinity very much; you were most likely taught that the Trinity is an impenetrable mystery that you will never understand, so you tuck it away as something not to be thought about. This is a pity, because the truth that there are three persons in one God is key to our ability to recognize God in the intimate relationship of married life.

Trinity helps us recognize God as a dynamic source of love and life. At the heart of the doctrine is the truth that God is in communion with the life he has created. He not only creates us as a Father might create, but also redeems us as Jesus did and empowers us to love one another as the Spirit empowers us. It's as if God lives a community life! The essence of God is a relationship of persons. Not only does this relational God love us, but this relational God is love in the world.

Therefore, we can find God in loving relationships around us: in the love of spouses for one another, and in the love of parents for children and grandchildren. Marriage is for us an open window to the divine. Because it is the closest and most intimate of loving relationships, it gives us the clearest picture of the relational, triune God.

In Jesus, we experience God as Emmanuel, translated "God among us." This experience may come in a spouse's loving care during illness or in a forgiving attitude toward the other's mistakes. It may be in the unity experienced in sexual love-making or in the mutual yielding to each other's preferences. The Trinity reveals God not as distant mystery but as loving presence within the intricate web of everyday relationships.

The Scriptures affirm this perception of God. In Genesis we are assured that "God created humankind in his image, in the image of God he created them; male and female he created them" (Genesis 1:27). Men and women image God together in their capacity for love and communion. Married life is the training ground for developing our capacity to love. In the first blush of married love, the desire for communion with each other stretches our potential for unity with another. As we build a life together over time, we are given more opportunities to realize our potential to love and experience union with another. Several years ago, I witnessed that in the neonatal intensive care unit of a hospital. A young father watched tearfully as the nurse turned his firstborn, a preemie son, in the incubator. He reached for the tiny hand, saying, "I never knew I could ever love anyone as much as I love this little guy."

A spirituality of marriage is based on the belief that God can be experienced in loving relationships. As John says in his letter to Christians, "No one has ever seen God; if we love one another, God lives in us" (1 John 4:12). "God is love, and those who abide in love abide in God, and God abides in them" (1 John 4:16). God is truly transcendent and beyond our ability to comprehend, but God is also immanent—as close to us as the love and unity we experience in our covenanted relationship. This is the key to marital spirituality, which rests on the possibility of being in communion with God by being in communion with others through the practice of self-giving love.

From *Familiaris consortio*

"God is love and in himself he lives a mystery of personal loving communion. Creating the human race in his own image and continually keeping it in being, God inscribed in the humanity of man and woman the vocation, and thus the capacity and responsibility, of love and communion. Love is therefore the fundamental and innate vocation of every human being." #11

God is present even when it seems to us that God is absent. In fact, the great saints and mystics testify that God is often working most powerfully in our lives when the times are darkest and God seems farthest away. They were not perfect, nor are we. Some days we love unselfishly, and some days we feel alienated and not-in-communion with anyone. God's presence is not dependent upon our attention to it.

Looking through a Clear Lens

Another helpful way of recognizing God's presence is to pay attention to and examine the picture we have in our imagination of the way God works. There is an old saying that "If you only have a hammer, everything looks like a nail." In other words, you are likely to see what you're looking for. If your mental picture of God is that of a trainer who gives you demanding tasks to accomplish, you will feel closest to him when you have done these deeds. If you see God primarily as a protector and nurturer, you will readily see him at work in the sacrifices parents make for their children, and in the gentle care of a wife for her ill husband.

The images of God that you and your spouse carry around in your heads have a powerful influence on the quality of the spiritual life you have as a couple. You may be only dimly aware of this if you rarely give much thought to your image of God. In fact, in my experience, spouses rarely talk to each other about their particular ideas about God and the way God works.

Some people see God as cold: distant, a harsh judge, an angry father, a scorekeeper. Others see God as warm: a faithful companion, shepherd, loving Father. Our ideas and images of God are deeply influenced by our parents, especially our fathers. A negative or dark image of God is an obstacle to spiritual life and growth. If a false image of an unloving, unforgiving, or distant God is ground into the lens you are looking through, your ability to see and experience the Divine within and around you will be greatly diminished. Now is the time to clear that lens, to seek out spiritual direction or do some good reading so that you can experience and appreciate the gift of God's presence.

Explore your image of God more deeply by doing the exercise below. The exercise offers a list of words you can use to describe God. Choose the words that fit best (remembering, of course, that words about God are mere metaphors), and discuss them with your spouse.

These words can help you probe your image of God more deeply. Separately, choose the words that best fit your image of God.

loving	condemning	master	powerful
forgiving	punishing	accountant	confusing
healing	gentle	protector	playful
creating	patient	savior	faithful
judging	comforting	knowing	other

What messages/images about God did you get as a child from your parents/other adults?

Separately, write your description or circle words above.

How is your image of God the same as your spouse's? How is it different?

Share with your spouse how you see each other's images of God either promoting or hindering recognition of God's presence in married life.

Seeing Married Life as a Spiritual Path

There is no single, easily definable model for marital spirituality because each of us experiences God in our own way. In marriage workshops I often ask couples to share a moment when they felt especially close to God as a couple. Some share a "religious" moment: a time of prayer with a couples' group, a retreat they made together, a special time at a Mass. Some couples share a moment connected with nature: a sunset while camping, a walk in a meadow on a starry summer night, a vista from the top of a mountain they climbed together. Other couples chose a moment involving people: a three-year-old saying grace at table, serving a meal at a homeless shelter, a disabled child who overcame an obstacle. Every couple will experience spirituality in a way that is unique to them.

But at the same time, I would suggest that the spirituality of marriage is marked by some common characteristics I have observed as couples reflect on their experience. We will focus on four of these characteristics.

- First, the cycle of growth in your marriage includes gains and losses, pleasure and pain—you will participate in the death and resurrection of Jesus as you move through married life. You will find God through suffering, waiting, and new life. Marital spirituality is *paschal*.
- Second, you will find God in your sexual relationship. Your bodies speak the language of love, and your union as man and woman reveals and makes present God's love in the world. Marital spirituality is *enfleshed*.
- Third, married love gives and nurtures life, and allows couples to participate in God's continuing creation. By

its nature, married love is procreative, generating life in the couple relationship, in children, and in the community. Marital spirituality is *generative*.

- Fourth, your failures in marriage will invite you to a process of forgiveness that mirrors God's own mercy and compassion. As an essential element of covenant living, forgiveness is a profoundly spiritual experience. Marital spirituality is *forgiving*.

We will look at these characteristics of couple spirituality in detail in an effort to help you explore your own unique spiritual experience of marriage.

How did the rose ever open its heart
and give to this world all its beauty?
It felt the encouragement of light against its being.
Otherwise, we all remain too frightened.

Hafiz, "It Felt Love"

7

How Married Love Grows

Seasons of Dying, Waiting, and Finding New Life

The gray skies and frozen ground of winter in the Midwest remind me of an important dimension of marriage. In fall the vibrant colors and rich harvest give way to a bleak scene. The garden and the yard look dead. Barren trees, lifeless flower beds, and frosted remains of shrubbery surround our home. I worry about the iris bulbs, the roots of the mum plants, and the delicate rose bushes. Will they survive the biting winds and frost?

They do. Each spring, when the earth begins to smell black and fertile, the small green shoots of the iris reappear, buds blossom on the trees, and the yucca plants are resurrected. Some have actually multiplied underground during their frigid hibernation. Life springs forth anew!

This seasonal rhythm in nature reflects a great truth at the heart of Christian belief—and at the heart of marital growth: new life and growth require some hibernation and dying. The dark and cold season of winter is a necessary part of the growth cycle in this part of the world. The hyacinth and tulips that bring such beauty in the spring would not arrive without a period of dormancy. They need winter in order to recover their potential for growth.

Marriage, like a garden, is a living thing, organic. Gardens and marriages are made up of seasons. Though some refer to marriage as a "state of life," we who have been married for many years know that it's not static but fluctuates between periods of rapid change, coasting, and near stagnation. Marriage is a process.

When two people promise to love each other forever, no matter what, they enter a process of learning and growth. When I said "I do" I really meant "I will"—that is, I will promise to learn how to love in this new covenant way. Over the years, my husband and I both had to let go of some of our original ideas about what married life would be. I see this in couples all the time. Betty learns that Steve isn't the financial whiz she thought he was and that a strict budget is necessary for them to survive. Tim learns that Jenny wasn't joking when she said she can't cook, so they have to share culinary responsibilities for the first years until she develops self-confidence in the kitchen.

Change and learning are essential to all human growth. Sometimes the learning in marriage is a matter of letting go of preconceived notions; other times it's a matter of discovering new skills and possibilities. The pattern of growth of most living things follows the pattern in the garden—a dying, a dormancy, and a flowering of new life.

All growth involves a kind of death. The seed contains the potential for the fruitful plant; to realize this potential, the seed must die. Jesus said that "unless a grain of wheat falls into the earth and dies, it remains just a single grain; but if it dies, it bears much fruit" (John 12:24).

The mystery of human growth follows the same rhythm common to growth in all living things. All of nature follows a rhythm of darkness and light. Early this morning the darkness was swallowed up by the light of dawn. The light of the sun triggers the biological process of growth in plants; darkness falls to bring cooling and rest. Seeds are buried in darkness and grow toward the light. Babies form in the rich hidden environment of the womb. Why should growth in marriage be an exception to this rhythm of darkness followed by light and new life?

We participate in a cycle of dying and rising, letting go and receiving new life on our lifelong journey. We die to the freedoms of the single life when we marry, but we gain deeper intimacy. We lose some of the free time together as a couple when we have our first child, but we cherish a new life to welcome and nurture. We let go of our children when they leave home but gain them back as life companions. Each stage of life has a transition time when the old way is gone but the new way hasn't been found. Waiting and darkness are necessary. Sorrow is the gateway to joy, and loss opens the hand to new gain.

Thus, one of four hallmarks of married spirituality is that it is paschal in nature. The word *paschal* means "to cross over." The root of the word is the word the Hebrew people used to describe their deliverance from slavery in Egypt. The enslaved people "crossed over" the Red Sea into freedom. The annual feast that celebrates this deliverance of the Jewish people is called Passover. The Christian Passover is the death and resurrection of Jesus— the suffering and death that crosses over into resurrected life.

The Paschal Mystery is reenacted every year in the Catholic liturgy. We observe Holy Thursday, remembering Jesus' final night with his disciples. And then come three uniquely defined days: Good Friday, Holy Saturday, and Easter Sunday. They lay out a pattern that we can apply to life in general and to marriage in particular. When we look honestly at our marriages, we see that they go through their own versions of Good Friday, Holy Saturday, and Easter Sunday.

> After the incarnation, we know that we are to look for God not in timeless glimpses of an angelic eternity, but at particular moments in particular places with their smells and sights, even places like Golgotha.
>
> WILLIAM L PORTIER, in *Tradition and Incarnation*

Good Friday

Every marriage has Good Fridays. A husband is injured on the job, leaving his wife to care for the family by herself for months. An elderly parent needs extensive care. A child falls very ill. One partner is suddenly laid off in a town with few other job opportunities. It's not hard to think of marriages with worse troubles than these. A biopsy reveals cancer. A baby is delivered stillborn. Couples face infertility and sometimes children die. Marriages are wracked by infidelity and addiction. Most of us know people who have suffered these terrible afflictions. Perhaps your own marriage has been touched by them.

With the eyes of faith, we view such a time of suffering as an experience of the cross. But we believe that, because of Jesus, the cross leads to new life. We don't really understand this mystery, and we don't understand how our marital Good Fridays share in the cross of Christ. Usually it's in looking back on our suffering or loss that we see how it opened the way to new life.

Jesus is our model for how to survive the cross: he gave himself over to it. When he saw that the cross was necessary, he embraced it. In faith and hope he turned to his Father for strength. To walk the path of the paschal mystery, it's first necessary to accept the reality of Good Friday. Jesus is our companion on the journey of marriage, experiencing everything we experience, including the utter depths of despair. There is no place we can go where Jesus has not gone before.

Consider the Good Fridays of your life. Recall together one
of the most difficult times of suffering or loss in your

marriage. What thoughts and feelings emerge as you remember this time or event?

How does looking upon that experience through the lens of paschal mystery (i.e., part of a cycle of change and growth) change your perception of it?

How did you experience Christ's presence with you during that time?

Holy Saturday

On Holy Saturday, Jesus' body lay in the tomb while those he loved despaired, losing hope in all that he had promised. All they could do was let the reality sink in that he was gone. They didn't know what would come next; they could not bear to think about the future. They could only wait and experience the darkness and the silence.

In marriage, we face uncertainty. We wait—in pain, fear, boredom, hopelessness—for something to happen. These are our Holy Saturdays, when all we can do is wait and hope.

Holy Saturday is dark, like the long days of winter when it appears that nothing is going on. But out of sight the natural world is simply dormant, its life still quite real in the roots and bulbs and seeds. Organisms are preparing for future growth.

With the eyes of faith, we can recall the Holy Saturdays of married life. A corporate buyout threatens a spouse's job—will she lose it, or not? A farm family goes deeper into debt because of a drought—should they continue to farm, or sell out? A child comes home late with the odor of marijuana on his clothes—is this experimentation, or the start of a serious drug habit? A child is diagnosed with a learning disability; what will the consequences be for the rest of her life? The answers aren't clear on Holy Saturday.

Sometimes Holy Saturday is a period of boredom or emotional distance between spouses. Other times it is a season of waiting and transition. We wait for a promotion or a desired pregnancy, or for military orders.

The church observes Holy Saturday as a time of holy waiting. The day is marked by sorrow and mourning. No Mass is celebrated. The statues in the church remain covered as they have during all of Lent. But Holy Saturday is also a time of expectant hope. While the earth waited, Jesus was energetically at work.

And so, although Holy Saturdays in your marriage might last for days or months, and although they are often marked by sorrow, they are also colored by hope. While we wait, God is energetically at work beneath the surface, unseen.

Consider the Holy Saturdays of your life. Recall together a time of transition or waiting in which you experienced uncertainty, insecurity, or darkness. What thoughts and feelings emerge as you remember this time?

How does looking at that time through the lens of paschal mystery change your understanding of it?

How did you experience Christ's presence with you during that time?

Easter Sunday

The paschal mystery is about redemption. The long cold night of winter ends and new life springs up in the garden. Light sweeps away darkness, and sorrow gives way to joy. Suffering ceases, and we rejoice. In marriage, too, we experience Easter again and again.

An Easter moment can be as simple as a weekend away alone together, away from jobs and kids, or reconciliation after a hurtful misunderstanding. Or the Easter moment can follow a much longer Good Friday and Holy Saturday. A spouse stays sober after the third time through treatment for alcoholism; a long-awaited pregnancy is achieved; patient work with a daughter with a learning disability is rewarded when she receives a scholarship to college.

In married life, the Good Friday–Holy Saturday–Easter Sunday pattern isn't just a metaphor but the reality of life's process. Every couple experiences this cycle in their own way; there is no uniform experience of this mystery of growth. As Christians, we recognize that death and suffering always have the potential of providing new life. We are not minimizing or sentimentalizing the real pain that has been or is still in our relationships, but we are trying to see that new life out of death is possible and that the steadfast love of God is present in the pain and in every stage of our growth, even when we cannot see it at the time.

Consider the Easter Sundays of your life. Recall a time of new possibilities, new life, great relief, or delight. What thoughts and feelings emerge as you remember these?

How does looking upon those experiences through the lens of paschal mystery change your perception of them?

How did you experience Christ's presence during those experiences?

In growing up as a child, what did you understand about the church's teaching regarding the paschal mystery of Christ?

In reflecting upon it now, what new insights do you have about this mystery that is at the heart of our faith?

From the Catechism

1085 [Christ's] Paschal mystery is a real event that occurred in our history, but it is unique: all other historical events happen once, and then they pass away, swallowed up in the past. The Paschal mystery of Christ, by contrast, cannot remain only in the past, because by his death he destroyed death, and all that Christ is—all that he did and suffered for all men—participates in the divine eternity, and so transcends all times while being made present in them all. The event of the Cross and Resurrection *abides* and draws everything toward life.

From the apostle Paul

Therefore we have been buried with him by baptism into death, so that, just as Christ was raised from the dead by the glory of the Father, so we too might walk in newness of life. For if we have been united with him in a death like his, we will certainly be united with him in a resurrection like his.
—Romans 6:4–5

8

How Married Love Gives Life
A Spirituality of Nurture

While sitting in church during the offertory at Sunday Mass, Sam suddenly understood his family life in a new way. While his wife Jenny took their fussing three-month-old son to the crying room and his three-year-old daughter played with a book of stickers, Sam's mind wandered to the day ahead. A litany of activities crossed his mind: brunch after Mass with friends, dinner at Jenny's parents' home later that day, all the preparations for a business trip the next day. Sam felt the week close in on him. He had promised to help the neighbors move and to do the grocery shopping to give Jenny a break. And he and Jenny had agreed to make space in their day for at least fifteen minutes of quiet conversation alone since their life was so hectic.

Just then, Sam watched as a young couple and their two children walked up the aisle and handed the gifts of water and wine to the priest standing in front of the altar. *I guess that's what I'm doing*, Sam thought, *handing over what I've got. And it doesn't seem like much right now.*

Sam and Jenny didn't feel very spiritual that morning, even though they were at Sunday Mass, but they were actually immersed in one of the great spiritual missions of marriage: the task of giving life. The obvious fruit of Sam and Jenny's conjugal love were their two children. But marital fruitfulness includes more than the rearing of children; it includes the common life they have together as a couple. Sam and Jenny understood how important this was, and they were committed to spending quality time alone. In addition to giving life to children and to their common life, the fruitfulness of marriage includes bringing life to the larger community. Sam and Jenny witnessed to this in their relationships with their community.

By its very nature, married love is generative, that is, life giving. Generativity is the second hallmark of marital spirituality. In the previous chapter we explored the first hallmark of marital spirituality—marriage's paschal dimension, by which we grow in holiness in a rhythm of death, waiting, and new life. Here we will see how the work of giving life to the marriage, to children, and to the community is a profoundly spiritual dimension of married love.

Creating a Common Life

Tom has a passion for hunting most weekends in the autumn. Marge loves curling up with a good book on a chilly fall day. She prefers a night of bridge with friends. He enjoys action movies.

In most marriages modern art meets the Dutch Masters, hot chili peppers meet up with quiche, and the always-be-on-time travels with the usually late. Opposites tend to be attracted to one another in marriage, which makes "two becoming one flesh" a challenge!

The invitation in marriage for two to become one flesh is a lifelong process of forming a partnership that honors differences while making sacrifices for the common good. The research of marriage experts shows that couples who have a sense of being an "us" have happier and more satisfying marriages. The Christian tradition maintains that the communion resulting from this becoming one is "a God thing": it is holy. But it is difficult to build a common life in a society that treasures individuality and autonomy as much as ours does.

Sexual union generates and strengthens the common life of a couple. It can literally "make love" happen between spouses. When spouses give themselves to each other in sexual union, they are creating a "communion of persons." This communion is a participation in the triune life of the Trinity. The unitive power of sexual intimacy is a great advantage couples have in the safety of an exclusive relationship. This communal life we make together is something new, a life that didn't exist before. Pope John Paul II described it beautifully, writing that marriage is "an intimate community of life and love."

The effort to build a common life in marriage isn't just about eating and sleeping in the same place, synchronizing calendars, and sharing in the care of children. These daily tasks create an environment for becoming one in mind and heart, but they can also create an environment for conflict or boredom.

Developing a "partnership of love and life," as Pope John Paul II described marriage, is a generative and deeply spiritual task, which means that God is at work in it. It requires understanding, care, humility, and self-sacrifice. The small daily efforts at heart-to-heart communication around differences, the thoughtful gestures during times of stress, the willingness to forgive faults that are irritating— all of these bring spouses into communion with one another. You and I become a "we." Our decisions, dreams, and plans are built around an "us" that slowly emerges over the years.

The glimpses of oneness we experience in marriage foreshadow what God has in store for us. Unity of heart and mind is the fruit of self-gift, and acts of self-gift such as Sam's offer to lighten Jenny's load at home manifest God's presence in the world.

The pressures on your common life can be especially intense in the early years of marriage. Research from the Creighton University's Center for Marriage and Family verifies what most couples experience. After children arrive, couples struggle to balance couple and parent time. Then the struggle gradually shifts to a conflict between work time and family time. As teens gain independence, parents have new pressures on their relationship, and the empty nest requires yet another adjustment to living together. Marriage is a process, and across the life cycle the "us" grows and is challenged by the pleasures and pressures of a growing family system of which it is a part.

Sam and Jenny, the couple at Sunday Mass, are squarely in the center of these pressures. An intimate community of life and love seems far off as Jenny anxiously supervises restless children and Sam nervously rehearses a business presentation while shopping for groceries.

But Sam and Jenny do some small things on a busy day to care for their common life. Their participation in the sacraments, particularly Sunday Eucharist, binds them together in Christ and strengthens them. In addition, they build community with family and friends. At brunch with their good friends they talk openly about the pressures they experience. They offer understanding and support to one another. Later, they go to Jenny's parents for dinner. Soon after they arrive, Jenny and Sam leave the children with their grandparents and take a leisurely twenty-minute walk together—quality "couple time" snatched from "parent time" and "family time."

On their walk, Sam and Jenny make plans to simplify their schedule so that the next weekend is more relaxing. These small choices to nurture their common life are one way in which they are generative and life giving.

Reflect for a moment and list several things you are doing as a couple at this stage in your marriage to create an "intimate community of love and life."

How do the privileges and responsibilities of nurturing life within your marriage relationship put you in touch with the Creator God?

From *Theology of the Body*

". . . man became the 'image and likeness' of God, not only through his own humanity, but also through the communion of persons which man and woman form right from the beginning." (46)

Giving Life through the Nurture of Children

A sleeping newborn baby, a dancing toddler, a confident kindergartener, an expressive grandchild, a beloved niece or nephew. Children are a gift! The new life of a child expands and energizes a family like nothing else!

From *Humanae vitae*

10. If we then attend to relevant physical, economic, psychological and social conditions, those are considered to exercise responsible parenthood who prudently and generaously decide to have a large family, or who, for serious reasons and with due respect to the moral law, choose to have no more children for the time being or even for an indeterminate period.

Responsible parenthood, moreoever, in the terms in which we use the phrase, retains a further and deeper significance of paramount importance which refers to the objective moral order instituted by God,—the order of which a right conscience is the true interpreter. As a consequence the commitment to responsible parenthood requires that husband and wife, keeping a right order of priorities, recognize their own duties towards God, themselves, their families and human society.

An essential generative dimension of married love is the potential for creating, sustaining, and nurturing the life of children. The procreative dimension of sexual intercourse connects us to our Creator God and gives us the privilege of cooperating with God in continuing the work of creation. For most couples this means giving birth to children. Couples who are not able to have their own children often express their procreative energy by adopting or fostering children. A couple married in later life express their creative energy by sponsoring foreign students for a semester at a time. Others who are not able to have children lend a supportive hand to poor or vulnerable children or children with special needs. Because so many children all over the world are without parents and the basic human necessities, the call to nurture and give life to children is especially urgent.

Parents create new life in partnership with God. We are "co-creators"; together we bring into being unique men and women with eternal destinies who play a distinct part in God's kingdom. "Be fruitful and multiply," God told the first parents. We do this through God's own creative power, which he freely shares with us. The last part of the "be fruitful" line in Genesis says "fill the earth and subdue it," which means not only populating the earth, but becoming stewards of life.

This is an awesome privilege and responsibility. We bring children into a world we will both introduce them to and protect them from. Responsible parenthood is more than birthing children. Unlike animals, who release offspring into a dangerous environment within a few months of birth, we humans nurture and protect life in order to help our children grow into the image of God they were meant to be.

We are stewards of the earth in the sense that we use it according to God's design in the service of life. Making responsible decisions about the number of children and the timing of their births is important and made possible with the assistance of natural family planning methods. These methods respect the sacred nature of fertility for those who are made in God's image, and they allow couples to "act in conformity with God's creative intention" (*Humanae vitae* 10).

Our sharing in God's creative power extends into the years of parenting. Raising children is spiritual work in the deepest sense. We are God's instruments as we nurture, educate, and socialize our children. Our parenting is an expression of the sacramental character of marriage. God is present to our children through us. He is more than present. Through us, God shapes and molds young men and women. A parent who is teaching a two-year-old not to bite his sister is teaching the fifth commandment and instilling a basic respect for the dignity of another person. It may not seem like spiritual work when we put a child in time-out or impose logical consequences on a wayward teen, but it is. Through small lessons and large interventions, our children grow into the men and women God intends them to be. Your marriage relationship itself is part of your child's spiritual formation. It gives them a glimpse of what God's love and fidelity must be like, even before they learn about God in formal religious education.

In family life, grace flows in the other direction as well. Parents form children spiritually, but children also form their parents. They transform us, making us into new people. Nothing expands a couple's capacity to love more powerfully than the challenge of having and raising children. During child rearing years, the partnership with our spouse is both challenged and strengthened. We learn to rely on God and other people instead of on ourselves alone. Children cause a drastic shift in priorities. Our priorities are measured most accurately by looking at the way we spend our time and money. For parents, an ever-increasing proportion of these scarce commodities are devoted to their children.

Parenting is God's school of virtue. In our roles as mothers and fathers we learn compassion, temperance, fortitude, self-sacrifice, humility, integrity, and forgiveness. In parenting we experience grief and joy and learn how to depend on God's limitless love when we meet the limits of our talents and resources.

Different spiritual gifts are called for at different times in our marriage and parenting years. When children are young, we need to be constantly attentive. When they are adolescents we learn to be patient and discerning. We will grow in courage and fortitude as we help our children face the challenges that come their way. Always there is the invitation to grow in the fundamental "theological" virtues: faith, hope, and love.

We are made in God's image, and parenting offers us the opportunity to grow in that image. Parenthood is a profoundly spiritual journey on an ordinary road. In the twenty-fifth chapter of Matthew's Gospel, Jesus depicts the multitudes assembled before him for judgment at the end of time. He welcomes into heaven those who served him: "For I was hungry and you gave me food, I was thirsty and you gave me something to drink, I was a stranger and you welcomed me, I was naked and you gave me clothing, I was sick and you took care of me, I was in prison and you visited me" (Matthew 25:35–36). This is what parents do. We feed our children, shelter them, clothe them, care for them when they are sick, and make a loving home for them, frequently unaware that these seemingly mundane actions are the litmus test for followers of Christ. Parents do these routine tasks out of love and fidelity to their children. By modeling these works of mercy in their home, parents teach their children how to show love and fidelity to others. In this way, Christian charity and the care of others emerges from the lived experience of the domestic church of the home. At the last judgment Jesus told the righteous "just as you did it for one of the least of these who are members of my family, you did it to me" (Matthew: 25:40). Our children are his children, and in serving them we serve and build up the body of Christ.

Reflect on the practical duties of parenthood or grandparenthood that are part of your life right now. How have you been shaped spiritually by your role as a caretaker of children?

Consider how parenting children is a participation in God's continuing creation. What makes it difficult to see the routine tasks of parenthood as spiritual work?

Complete the Homemade Holiness exercise in Appendix 1 on page 191. Answer the two questions at the end.

If you are not parenting children at this time, how might you be generative or procreative in your relationships with the children around you?

Giving Life in Your Community

How do you serve the life of the community? By mowing a neighbor's lawn, volunteering in the parish, assisting a candidate for political office, or participating in a neighborhood recycling program. Is there an elder neighbor or friend who lives alone and needs a visit or a ride to church? Does your city have a homeless shelter or domestic violence shelter that needs support? In serving the life of the community, we look to help the poor and vulnerable, the sick and marginalized.

To be fully generative, a couple's love must spill out into the larger human family. People are living longer, and increasing numbers of couples are married forty years or more. Active child rearing takes up only part of married life. But the procreative purpose of sexual intercourse continues past the childbearing years. In his teachings on the theology of the body, John Paul II emphasizes the importance of maintaining a "definite family and procreative attitude" (*Theology of the Body*, 399). Whether during times of periodic chastity for the purpose of regulating births of children or after menopause, married couples are still called by their vocation to cooperate with God in the ongoing work of creation. To be procreative also means that we support life wherever it is vulnerable or needs assistance: the unborn, sick, poor, elderly, immigrants, and refugees. This includes protecting the life of the Earth whose resources are necessary for human life.

When a couple is "pro" creation, it means they respect all human and natural life at every stage. There is a sense of stewardship about all of creation that is nurtured by the security and stability that a satisfying married life provides.

Having babies is the natural creative end of married love, and caring for them is truly a work of stewardship. But there is a point at which the kids have left the house, or before they have been born, when spouses can utilize their energy and gifts to serve the community that surrounds them. A newly married couple who is postponing a first child while finishing their education makes a weekly visit to their homebound grandmother. A retired couple volunteers at a day-care center for low-income children. Physical fertility may be limited by the biological clock, but a married couple can be procreative until their last breath.

Serving the life of the community is not an option for Christians; it is a Gospel imperative. A not-so-surprising advantage is that couples say that such community service done as an "us" unites them in a special way and enriches their own life.

When we say that married spirituality is generative, we reflect on three dimensions of generativity: creating a common life and forming an "us"; giving life and supporting the lives of children; and being procreative in the larger community.

At this time in your marriage, how are you giving life in the three areas mentioned above?

- your common life together
- your life with children
- giving life to the larger community

Name one thing you can do to become more aware of the spiritual nature of these ordinary life-serving dimensions of generativity.

9

Sex and Spirituality
How Marriage Brings the Two Together

A warm welcome home embrace. Sleeping like spoons. A gentle back rub. The soft skin of a baby's cheek against yours. A kiss of blessing from father to daughter on her wedding day. These are some of the countless physical expressions of love and affection that we enjoy in our married lives. Physical expressions of love are an important part of the spirituality of marriage. To a great extent, we accomplish through our bodies the profound spiritual unity to which we are called in marriage.

This is a third characteristic of marital spirituality. We have seen how our growth in marriage follows a rhythm of death and new life, drawing us into the paschal mystery of Jesus Christ. We have seen how our marriage is generative—a union that creates, nurtures, and sustains life. Here we will reflect on the physical character of marriage. Marital spirituality involves our bodies. It is enfleshed.

We commonly understand spirituality as the realm of reality that is not material or tangible. We access it through prayer and the practice of virtue. When asked to describe their spirituality, most couples will mention the sacraments, going to Mass, reading the scriptures, and engaging in personal and family prayer.

Prayer and the sacraments are essential to everyone, married or single, but in Christian marriage the spiritual also involves the body. We express love for each other physically. We cradle babies and hug our children. We kiss and embrace. Above all, husbands and wives make love. What we do with our bodies is a crucial part of our call to holiness as married people.

This is obvious in one sense, and we have been talking about it throughout this book. The Catholic perspective is sacramental. God entered our physical world in the incarnation of Christ; the things of this physical world reveal God and lead us to God. In the Catholic tradition, marriage is one of the special sacraments by which God's power, presence, and grace enter our lives. And it is the vehicle through which God is present to you and your spouse and, through you as a couple, to the world.

Marriage is a union of many things: our hopes and dreams, our finances, our destinies, our ambitions, and our time. But it is first of all a union of our bodies. In Genesis, we read that God's design for his creation is that "the two shall become one flesh." The Catholic Church teaches that this bodily union is essential for the sacrament; in fact, sexual intercourse consummates the marriage covenant. Without this union of bodies, a marriage is not recognized as a valid sacrament.

However, in another sense, the spiritual importance of what we do with our bodies is not so obvious. Our culture has cheapened and degraded sexuality. The separation of body and spirit is such a deeply ingrained habit that it often seems as if the bedroom is the last place we expect to find spirituality. Yet, our sexuality itself is another means of knowing God.

How Faith Changes the Way We See Sex

After their third baby, Nancy was sleep-deprived and over-whelmed. She needed rest and some time to herself but was not interested in sex. Ted was also stressed and tired, but when Nancy rejected his advances he took it personally. Even with the joy of their new child, they felt less intimately connected and less loved than ever before.

Every couple has gone through times like this, and most couples have felt the strain caused by the lack of physical inti-macy. Sexual intercourse and the variety of tender physical expressions of love between spouses are fundamental to mari-tal intimacy. Sexual loving and affectionate expression have the power to unite and comfort spouses. In the arms of our beloved we can experience acceptance and safety. We can be vulnerable and open. The pleasures of sex can reveal a divine reality. The feeling of ecstatic oneness that comes with marital lovemaking is a deeply spiritual experience, a metaphor for God's desire to be one with us. When we make love, we are in a very direct way participating in the mystery of God.

This mystery of sexuality was explored by Pope John Paul II in his "Theology of the Body," a series of 129 lectures that he delivered at weekly audiences in Rome between 1979 and 1984. John Paul's ideas represent a profound development in Catholic theological thinking about marriage. He developed his ideas in great detail and expressed them in sometimes opaque language, but some of his observations are helpful here.

A central thesis of the theology of the body is that "the body, and it alone, is capable of making visible what is invisible." This is a deep truth about Christian revelation. God entered the world in the person and the body of the man Jesus of Nazareth—the spiritual is revealed in the physical; heaven comes to earth; the body reveals the spirit. The most fundamental fact about our bodies is that they come in two genders, male and female. In fact almost all living things come in male and female genders, which come together sexually to reproduce the species. This says something important about God. The book of Genesis says that "God created man in his image. . . . male and female he created them." If this is so, then the coming together of man and woman in the most intimate of human acts says something important about God as well.

John Paul II called this "the nuptial meaning of the body." That is, as part of the very design of creation, we are physically constructed to image God and participate in God's creative power. When we make love, we exercise this creative power by establishing a new union in "one flesh with the capacity to create a new life." This is God's design. Says John Paul, spouses "have the capacity of expressing . . . that love in which the person becomes a gift and by means of this gift fulfills the meaning of his existence" (65).

The body speaks a type of "language," according to John Paul. Through our sexual union, God is proclaiming his generous love and care for us and is making this present through the generous self-giving of the lovers. This is why being intentional about nurturing a healthy sex life in marriage and addressing problems when they arise is intimately connected to our relationship with God.

Lower animals have sex instinctually. Theirs is a purely physical function satisfying a biological purpose. It is expressed randomly without reference to relationship or love. Much of the sex displayed in the media reflects this kind of instinctual sex drive.

But *making love* is a uniquely human act. Human beings have the capacity for friendship and self-giving. Humans can desire the good of another person because of love. They can choose how to make love, and what the lovemaking means. Human lovemaking can of course resemble the barnyard sex of animals. It can be primarily a surrender to an urge that satisfies a personal appetite. Or it can be a deeply intimate union that satisfies appetite while expressing each partner's desire to give the gift of oneself to the other. The way partners make love expresses their desire for the good of the other.

This self-giving in human lovemaking in the context of a covenant relationship touches on God's self-giving expressed in Jesus Christ. Because of his love for us, Jesus emptied himself completely, his life and his death perfectly demonstrating God's boundless love for us. We do this, though imperfectly, for each other in our marriages. We do it in a thousand ways, large and small, day after day, year after year, but we are never so open and so vulnerable to each other as we are when we make love. That is why great mystical writers often describe their experience of intimacy with God in the language of married sexual love. The Bible itself uses this language in the collection of love poems known as the Song of Songs, which begins:

> Let him kiss me with kisses of his mouth!
> More delightful is your love than wine!
>
> Your name spoken is a spreading perfume—
> that is why the maidens love you.

Draw me!—
We will follow you eagerly!
Bring me, O king, to your chambers.
With you we rejoice and exult,
we extol your love; it is beyond wine:
how rightly you are loved!

In his book *The Holy Longing*, Ronald Rolheiser describes Christian sexuality this way: "Sexuality is a beautiful, good, extremely powerful, sacred energy, given us by God and experienced in every cell of our being as an irrepressible urge to overcome our incompleteness, to move toward unity and consummation with that which is beyond us." Counter to the media's notion of sex, couples who hold this posture toward their sexuality are able to understand chastity in a way others cannot. To be chaste in marriage is to reverence sexuality for what it truly is and to view sexual loving as something other than self-gratification or recreation.

Sexual loving takes us outside ourselves. On our better days, it places us at the service of another in an attitude of generosity and radical openness. Though our bodies may seem at times to be an obstacle to divine presence, they are actually the vehicles through which God reveals his presence and his love for us. Sexual intimacy in the context of the covenant of marriage is sacramental—a sign of God's love, and it's a sign that brings about what it signifies. It's an aspect of God's creation that we can thoroughly enjoy and delight in. And God said, "It is good!"

While drawing spouses together into physical and spiritual communion, sexual intimacy gives couples the privilege of cooperating with God in bringing new life into the world in children.

Both the unitive and procreative dimensions of sexual intercourse are essential to sacramental marriage.

Not all couples are physically able to conceive and birth children, but those who do have witnessed the indescribable joy that comes with seeing the fruit of your own love born into the world as baby boy or girl. When seen with the eyes of faith, every act of intercourse is an opportunity for both a physical communion that gives life to the couple and an opportunity to cooperate with God in creating new life in children. The invitation in Genesis to "be fruitful and multiply, fill the earth" is meant to be realized in the safe and secure nest woven over time by men and women in covenant love.

Consider the ways love is enfleshed in your marriage, including sexual and sensual expressions such as a parting kiss or touch, an embrace, a back rub, and so on.

What experiences of "enfleshed love" have been windows to the divine for either or both of you? What do those experiences reveal to you about God's love for you?

In what ways do these experiences enrich or clarify your image of God and God's design for creation?

Why Sex and Spirituality Have Become So Disconnected

If the conjugal union of married couples is such a powerful manifestation of God's love, then why is there so much negativity, confusion, and anxiety connected with sex? To some married couples, the theology of the body seems to have little to do with the actual reality of their sexual lives.

One reason is that sexual problems are common in marriage, and church documents often portray a sexual ideal that many couples cannot relate to. Like the paschal rhythm of growth in all things, sexual intimacy and growth for couples includes times of loss, waiting, and uncertainty along with joy and new life. The patterns of sexual intimacy in marriage are subject to changes in the life cycle. For a period of time before and after childbirth, sexual satisfaction plummets for many couples. There are times of boredom or crisis when sexual intercourse is difficult or impossible. Certain medications, periods of depression or illness, or stress can interrupt the flow of sexual energy between spouses. Most couples find it hard to talk about sex and to give it the proper attention it deserves or to seek out help when sex becomes a source of hurt and alienation. Most find it very hard to think about their sexual lives in spiritual terms. Couples are not usually encouraged to see sex as a gift that must be nurtured and developed in order to be experienced as a participation in the divine plan of creation.

Another reason we find it difficult to connect sex with spirituality is that the treatment of sexuality by contemporary culture has deeply affected the way we think about it. There's nothing mysterious or spiritual about the sexuality that surrounds us—sex is imagery for advertising, a recreational sport for beautiful young people, a titillating topic for entertainment, and a commodity that pornographers sell on the Internet. Sex is portrayed as a powerful animal urge that must be satisfied. Efforts to place boundaries on sexual activity or to discuss it with reverence and respect are greeted with derision, and the exclusivity and permanence that come with Christian marriage are seen by some as quaint. As Christians, we may reject this treatment of sex, but it nevertheless shapes our environment and influences us in many ways. It's very hard to think about sex as something holy when the sexuality we see around us has become a consumable product and a means of transforming people into objects for enjoyment.

We rightly resist the media portrayal of sex, but it's possible to get stuck in a predominately negative, reactive mode. Sex can bring great comfort, pleasure, joy, companionship, and deep, meaningful union between a couple and within a family. It can also bring sorrow: broken hearts, ruined marriages, disease, abortion, obsession, and bad life decisions. Sexual addiction to pornography has become a serious issue in many marriages. These real problems can loom large in our minds and color our thinking about sex. Dwelling on the havoc that sex can wreak makes it difficult to appreciate the happiness it can bring and its profound spiritual significance. A positive vision of the meaning of sexuality can be an antidote to this negative portrayal of sex.

Another reason we experience a disconnect between our sexuality and our spirituality is the perception that the Catholic Church is concerned primarily with the *problems* of sexuality. The church's teaching seems focused on difficult issues such as contraception, abortion, homosexuality, masturbation, in vitro fertilization, and other moral issues that have to do with sexuality and reproduction. To some degree, this is a distorted impression fostered by our culture and media. The church's attitude toward sexuality is very different from that of secular culture. These differences flow from a positive, life-enhancing theology of sexuality, but the church's prohibitions get far more attention than does its affirmative teaching. The media like stories. And when it comes to sex, the compelling story is the tale of right-thinking good-hearted ordinary people pitted against repressive clergy and religious institutions.

Yet it's also fair to say that many of the church's pastors and teachers have had an uncertain grasp of the spiritual potential of sexuality. For centuries Catholic teaching on sex was influenced by the philosophical view that the body and spirit are at odds. This world was seen as a pale and tragically flawed reflection of an ideal world that existed somewhere in the "heavens" or in the mind of God. The immortal soul was imprisoned within a sinful body, and the realm of the spirit was firmly separated from the realm of the flesh. To grow spiritually, one had to master the demands of the body. It was especially important to overcome sexual desires, which were seen as particularly dangerous to spiritual health.

We've seen a shift toward a more balanced, incarnational spirituality in recent decades. Pope John Paul II's theology of the body is an important component of this change, as is the shared reflection of married couples. Sexuality is seen as something good, something to delight in because it comes from God and reveals God's love. Nevertheless, traces of the old mistrust and fear of the body and of sexual pleasure linger. It will take a long time for renewed appreciation of the spiritual significance of sexuality to permeate the Catholic consciousness.

For all these reasons we have difficulty seeing sex in spiritual terms. Most of us have difficulty grasping the fact that our lovemaking reveals the love of God. These difficulties underscore the radical character of the gospel. We can grow so accustomed to the central tenets of the Christian faith that we forget how remarkable they are. It's an extraordinary thing that God became man and experienced all the messy realities of our human condition. It's extraordinary that Jesus saved us by dying. We forget, as St. Paul wrote, that the cross is a scandal and an outrage. Jesus comes to us in the form of ordinary bread and wine. The water of baptism initiates us into new life. And our lovemaking brings God into our bedroom.

What messages were you given/taught about sexual loving in marriage? From whom did you learn them?

Which messages contributed to a disconnect between sex and spirituality?

Which messages opened you to the spiritual significance of sexual loving?

What Can Happen to
Make Love Better

If sexuality in marriage is fundamental to spirituality, then we would expect Catholic couples to work as hard on attending to their sexual lives as they do on their finances, on prayer, child rearing, schedule planning, and other important aspects of married life. Some couples do, but in my experience, most do not. Even couples who thoroughly discuss other areas of their lives together are often silent about sex.

This isn't surprising, given the disconnect between spirituality and sexuality in our contemporary culture. We're acutely aware of sexual temptations and sexual sin, and we're surrounded by false but potent images of sex in the media. Thus, sex can come to be associated more with shame and guilt than with communion and self-giving. Some avoid the topic of sex because they are unaware of its power—or afraid of its power.

Every couple's sexual life is unique—no part of marriage is more exclusively and distinctively your own than your lovemaking. Some common understandings about sex can guide your reflection and conversation.

Sex is good.

Not only is sex good, but it is a *great* good. It is good because it is "of God." Our sexuality is an essential dimension of being human. Because we are made in God's image and likeness, we are made good—not perfect, but as Genesis says, "God saw everything that he had made, and indeed, it was very good." (Genesis 1:31). As Catholic Christians we believe in original sin* but we also believe

---

*By original sin the church means that because of our fellowship in the human race through physical descent, we are born without that special relationship with God which is called grace [cf. Trent, Sess V, canons 1–4].

that human life in its physical, psychological, and spiritual dimensions is fundamentally good.

One of the ways we as human persons can encounter God in marriage is through our bodily union. When sexual love-making emerges from a desire for unity with one another and a desire to give self to the other, it mirrors divine self-giving. In this way, sexual union is not only good but it also has the potential for being holy.

When couples gather to reflect on this teaching, they know intuitively from their experience of sexual intimacy that it is good and that this experience is one of transcendence; there is something so profound about the ecstasy of being one together, but they do not have words to describe its sacred character. They are reluctant to call it a "spiritual" thing, let alone a "holy" action, but they know it can be sacred space for them.

Because the language around sexuality has been cheapened and trivialized in popular culture, couples now need a whole new vocabulary if they are to express the deeper meaning of their sexual union. In his reflections on the theology of the body, John Paul II has given us some language to begin exploring the depths and goodness of our sexuality.

Catholics are more open about sex than we were a generation ago. But we have barely begun to understand the spiritual implications of seeing sexuality as a sacramental sign of God's presence. This is a powerful incentive for married couples to devote the time and energy necessary to attend their sexual lives. Many blessings await those who do.

Growth in sexual intimacy is paschal.

Our sex lives, like marriage as a whole, participate in the paschal mystery of Jesus' life, death, and resurrection. Sex is a mixture of light and darkness, grace and peril, joy and sorrow, struggle and triumph. Lovemaking can be a transcendent experience of the greatest pleasure. But lovemaking can also be unrewarding, difficult, even hurtful.

We should expect these difficult times and not be discouraged by them. They are part of the paschal drama played out on Good Friday, Holy Saturday, and Easter Sunday. The recurrence of problems and difficulties in our sexual lives is all the more reason to speak about sex honestly and to make choices that bring freshness and new life to sex.

Sex is a gift.

Our ability to give ourselves to our spouse through sexual love is an astonishing gift. It leads to the deepest intimacy, and it is the source of the greatest pleasure and delight. It can be a window to the divine desire for unity with creation. Looking at our sexuality with gratitude moves us to do all that we can to experience the fullness of something so powerful and so precious.

Though we have focused here mostly on sexual intercourse, sexuality encompasses the entire spectrum of human gender with all of the differences and commonalities of male and female. Sexual intimacy, and the vulnerability it requires, is only one dimension of our sexual sensual selves designed by God to bring us into union with him and with one another. The faithful promise of unconditional love and acceptance, which marriage provides, allows us the safety to grow in vulnerability and deeper union with one another.

Achieving a positive attitude about sex may require changing negative messages, healing negative past experiences, gathering new information, or seeking professional help. And, as in all other areas of marital growth, bringing our hopes and needs about sex to God in prayer can be a source of grace and comfort.

In your marriage, how might you better integrate the above reflections: sex is good, sex is gift, sexual growth is paschal?

How Sex Is a Form of Communication

Like a good conversation with your spouse or a joint prayer to God, sex is a means of communication in marriage.

Sometimes our words fail us when we try to communicate our deepest emotions. We often resort to poetry or gifts to express ourselves adequately. At such times, sexual loving in the form of touch or embrace are ways couples communicate with each other without words. Building a marriage that is a "partnership of love and life" is not possible without communication. Because marriage is a covenant between spouses and God, the covenant relationship also requires the ability to communicate between spouses and God. I refer to that communication with the divine that nourishes the marriage covenant as couple prayer.

In talking with couples as they explore both prayer and sex in their experience of marriage, I notice some similarities that may be helpful to you in understanding the spiritual dimension of sexuality.

- **Both are forms of intimate communication.** We shouldn't underestimate how much we say to each other through the language of sex. Sometimes we say with our bodies what cannot even be translated into words, just as prayer can be a powerful connection with God even when we cannot put into words what we feel or desire.
- **Both are sources of power and strength.** The energy that generates between lovers translates into increased passion and enthusiasm for all of life. The unity between

spouses that flows from a common prayer life enables them to face challenges with more confidence and endurance.

- **Both can bring ecstasy but sometimes require work and thoughtfulness.** And sometimes what begins as work turns into ecstasy! Whether in prayer or in love-making, there are times when the hardest thing to do is settle down and begin, but before long we are in a beautiful flow of passion, embrace, and tenderness.

- **Both require a kind of nakedness before the other.** Prayer deepens as we learn to come before God as we really are, with illusions and delusions stripped away. Our sexual union deepens when, along with our physical nakedness, we take off our defenses, our masks, and our expectations.

- **Both can be used to manipulate the other.** We distort the act of prayer when we try to bend God to our will, to bargain with God, or when we do all the talking. We distort the act of love when we use sex selfishly to satisfy our own desires. Good prayer and good sex are acts of giving and receiving.

- **Both can be spontaneous but often require thought and planning.** Especially as our lives develop—with careers, children, and other responsibilities—it becomes more of a necessity to plan the activities that are a priority to us. Two of our most important activities are communion with God and with each other. Making plans to have sex may not seem romantic, but it may be necessary during some seasons of marriage. The same is true of couple prayer.

- **Both nourish a covenant relationship.** Prayer and sex foster steadfast fidelity and take us into the deepest intimacies with another within the context of an exclusive covenant relationship. The marriage covenant mirrors God's covenant with his people. Prayer and sexuality are the languages of committed love.

Which of the seven commonalities demonstrates most clearly for you how sex and spirituality are intertwined?

10

Forgiveness and Reconciliation
What Makes Covenant Love Possible

There's the car returned home with an empty tank, and the fines from illegal parking, the dishes left on the countertop, and two overdraws from the checking account in one week. A forgotten anniversary, a nasty criticism in front of friends. How many ways can people who love each other be careless, hurtful, and insensitive? The possibilities are endless.

The fourth and final characteristic of marital spirituality is the one that makes it possible to live together long-term. This is the willingness of spouses to forgive one another and their ability to reconcile differences. Not only is forgiveness crucial to married life, but it is also central to the gospel itself. When Jesus explained the gospel to his disciples in an appearance after his resurrection, he said that he suffered, died, and rose so that "repentance for the forgiveness of sins, would be preached in his name to all the nations, beginning from Jerusalem." Without God's forgiveness, we are lost and alienated from ourselves and one another. Without mutual forgiveness between spouses, marriages would crumble.

Husbands and wives who develop habits of forgiveness and learn how to live with each other's differences become better life partners and are happier. They avoid deep-seated resentment and anger that erode feelings of love and affection. Forgiveness and reconciliation are spiritual disciplines that we acquire in the gritty, sometimes harsh reality of daily life together. We forgive because we love. As the Catechism of the Catholic Church puts it: "Forgiveness . . . bears witness that, in our world, love is stronger than sin" (2844).

An attitude of realism and humility makes forgiveness much easier. I once attended a bridal shower at which the married women were invited to share a pearl of wisdom with the bride-to-be. One woman shared a habit that had served her particularly well: "Every morning I get out of bed, stand in front of the bathroom mirror, take a hard look at myself and say, 'You ain't no prize either.'"

The Necessity of Forgiveness

Matt and Denise knew each other in grade school and were engaged for a year before they were married. Still, within weeks of their wedding they were at serious odds.

Denise: Matt got angry all the time. While we were dating, I admired his passion. I liked his energy and zeal. After we were married, he would lose his temper when something happened that he didn't like. He would yell at me and stomp out of the room. Matt frightened me. My father used to terrify the family with his anger—I couldn't bear the thought of spending my life with an angry husband.

Matt: Denise is a well-organized and disciplined person, more so than me. I like that quality in her, but I didn't like it so much when she criticized me. I didn't take care of the car. I left things lying around the apartment. I didn't stick to our budget. I felt like I was a little kid again, getting a lecture from my mother. I gave Denise a hard time, until we started to talk about it.

Matt and Denise began their reconciliation by agreeing not to label each other. Matt stopped calling his wife a "control freak," and Denise stopped calling her husband a "crazy madman." They stopped making negative generalizations ("You're an angry man." "You're being critical again.") and started talking about how certain behaviors affected them ("That frightens me." "I feel humiliated when you say that."). They came to understand how their reactions to each other echoed hurtful childhood memories. They asked each other for forgiveness—they asked explicitly, and they were as specific as possible about the behavior they wanted to change.

Matt and Denise's story is hardly unique. Partners who promise to love and honor each other on their wedding day often criticize and ignore each other a few weeks later. They insist on having their own way, and they whine or yell when they can't. They stomp out of rooms. They show up late, forget about promises, and lose important things. They are sloppy or crude in each other's presence. They are demanding, boring, or they never shut up.

Have I included every offensive thing married people do? Hardly. Every person is unique and has his or her own way of being offensive and taking offense. All of these flaws and imperfections will be on display in marriage. In the most intimate of relationships, nothing can be hidden for long. In marriage we will have abundant opportunities to forgive and be forgiven, running the gamut from sexual infidelity to tracking grease from the garage floor into the kitchen. It's fair to say that no one in their right mind would say the marriage vows—that "I will be true to you in good times and bad"—unless they really believed that forgiveness was possible. The fact is, a covenant needs forgiveness because you cannot possibly do what you promised.

For yourself, what happenings or situations are most offensive or hurtful to you?

How would your spouse answer this question?

What is your personal approach to handling hurt or differences? What is your first step?

What do you do when your approach seems not to be working?

The Benefits of Forgiveness

Couples who master the art of forgiveness reap psychological, physical, and spiritual rewards. Perhaps the most obvious is psychological and emotional freedom; couples who do not learn to forgive store up a load of resentments over the years. The resentments can involve serious matters, such as lying about money and disagreements about handling children. Or they can simply be the by-product of differences in personality and taste. One woman I know resented the fact that her husband liked only action-packed crime and thriller movies and didn't even pretend to be interested in the romantic comedies she liked. He, in turn, resented her taste in home decorating. He never invited his friends over to watch sports because he thought their den looked like a museum.

We're often inclined to avoid dealing with these matters. The big issues look too big and too dangerous to deal with, while the small matters are "no big deal." We think we can sweep them under the rug and go on with life. But unresolved and often unacknowledged conflicts lead to resentment, and resentments can burrow themselves deeply into marriage, weakening our love for each other and sapping our spiritual strength. The little problems we've swept under the rug fester and grow and turn into a massive lump of hurt and anger. Actress Carrie Fisher is credited as having said, "Resentment is like drinking poison and waiting for the other person to die." Married couples who learn to forgive are freed from this terrible emotional burden.

Forgiveness has physical benefits too. Resentment can literally poison our bodies. Chronic anger and resentment are associated with a host of ailments, including high blood pressure, heart problems, substance abuse, and depression. Forgiveness leads to better overall health.

However, the greatest benefits of forgiveness are spiritual rewards. Resentment blinds us to the good in other people. It inhibits our capacity to give and receive love. Resentment damages the covenant you made on your wedding day, and it injures the "us" that you and your spouse are working to create. Resentment and anger create a "hardened heart" that silences the voice of God in our lives.

Difficulties will inevitably challenge your marriage, but the means to deal with them are near at hand. The model for Christian marriage is the covenant between Yahweh and Israel—a covenant that was in constant need of repair. The Hebrew people repeatedly violated the covenant: they dallied with pagan gods, oppressed the poor, treated strangers brutally, and otherwise trampled on their covenant promises. Yahweh constantly forgave them, receiving the people back despite their egregious failures. When the Hebrew people looked back, they understood that God's steadfast love was the most outstanding fact about their long history as a people. When Jesus instituted the new covenant, he did so at a Passover supper, the Jewish annual ritual of remembering God's steadfast fidelity and forgiving love. Jesus gave us the new covenant in the context of forgiveness; at the Last Supper he said, "for this is my blood of the covenant, which will be shed on behalf of many for the forgiveness of sins."

Forgiveness given out of love is the glue that holds marriage together when anger and hurt put stress on it. Although it's painful to deal with offenses and forgive them, and resolving resentment may seem like messy work, it is an essential spiritual exercise that strengthens and preserves the marriage covenant.

Forgiveness is a gift that we give each other day in and day out, when we're deeply offended or just "fed up." It's a gift we give ourselves, because forgiveness is essential for good health and spiritual maturity.

God is generous and steadfast in his love for us. Nowhere do we see this more clearly than in a marriage that is marked by mutual forgiveness. Marital spirituality is forgiving.

Describe a situation in your marriage when you asked for and received forgiveness. In looking back on the situation, in what way did your relationship benefit?

When your heart is "hardened" toward your spouse, how does it affect your attitude and behavior?

The Impact of Forgiveness upon Intimacy and Spirituality

None of this is easy. Marriage is a process and a paradox. It takes time for spouses to achieve intimacy with each other, and doing so means learning about and coming to terms with each other's flaws. Thus the paradox: to stay alive and spiritually healthy, a marriage must keep growing, and this growth comes about, in part, through each partner challenging the other to grow in generosity, patience, humility, and the other virtues. Yet intimacy and spiritual health also require that we accept ourselves and our partner as we are, both blessed and broken. This is a fine line to walk. When does challenging our partner become discontented nagging? When does acceptance become resigned indifference? Every couple faces this challenge, and it's impossible to meet it without a mature capacity for forgiveness.

It took Matt and Denise time to develop a level of intimacy that allowed them to face their hurts honestly and openly with each other. Most couples don't start out with that degree of intimacy. The normal relationship cycle of growth moves from infatuation through disillusionment to intimacy. Most partners are infatuated with each other at the beginning of their relationship; they have an unrealistic view of each other. Each sees the other as the person who will make life complete, who fills up all the empty spaces. This is the way that Matt and Denise felt about each other through their months of courtship and engagement. Denise had the orderly mind that Matt admired, and Matt had a creative energy that Denise wanted for herself.

One tricky aspect of infatuation is that it can feel like intimacy. Infatuated couples delight in each others' presence, spending as much time together as they can. They are excited and thrilled to discover a "soul mate" who supplies what is lacking and who fulfills their dreams. But infatuation is not intimacy; it is romantic appeal, usually energized by a strong current of sexual attraction that tugs powerfully at the emotions. Men and women do not see each other clearly when they are infatuated with each other. Nevertheless, infatuation is an important stage in marriage; most couples wouldn't make it to the altar unless they were infatuated with each other to some extent.

As a relationship develops, infatuation usually is followed by disillusionment, a kind of "dark night" of the relationship. Disillusionment is the painful realization that the romantic picture of the beloved is flawed. Married life together brings out the other person's defects. In fact, often the very qualities that caused infatuation when couples were dating look very different under the pressure and scrutiny of marriage. Matt loved Denise's discipline and sense of order when they were getting to know each other, but later those traits began to annoy him, especially when he felt he was being controlled by her. When they were dating, Matt's passionate nature opened thrilling new experiences for Denise, but when she lived with him, she saw anger, impatience, and other less desirable aspects of his passion.

The arrival of the disillusionment stage is a critical turning point in marriage. In one direction lie bitterness and failure. Partners think, *Maybe I married the wrong person.* They might begin to look for someone who they think would be a better match. Disillusionment can start a process that leads to divorce—many times it triggers a process of emotional separation. The fun-loving guy can be irresponsible; the determined woman can be nagging and resentful. Spouses can react to these surprises by becoming wary, by withdrawing into their private emotional worlds. A disillusioned man once told his therapist, "I was happier when I was single. I was by myself—and sure, I felt lonely, but it wasn't as miserable as being together, yet alone."

But if they choose, couples can work at forgiving each other's limitations and faults, acknowledging and working through the disillusionment. This is profoundly spiritual work. In doing this, they come to truly understand and love one another more deeply.

This is what Matt and Denise did. They were disillusioned with each other, but instead of warily and sadly withdrawing from each other they forgave one another for not living up to certain expectations, and they acknowledged their difficulties, resolving to work through them. Doing so took time and work, but the rewards were great. They achieved an intimacy that was far deeper and more satisfying than the infatuation that carried them through their courtship and first months of marriage. This cycle of growth from infatuation to disillusionment to intimacy continues over time. Intimacy often leads to a new infatuation with the beloved, a more realistic infatuation that gives energy to the relationship. This intimate acceptance of the other with all his or her faults is a profoundly spiritual experience. It renews the covenant of marriage. When couples do this, they give to each other a glimpse of God's acceptance of us as we are.

Relationship Cycle

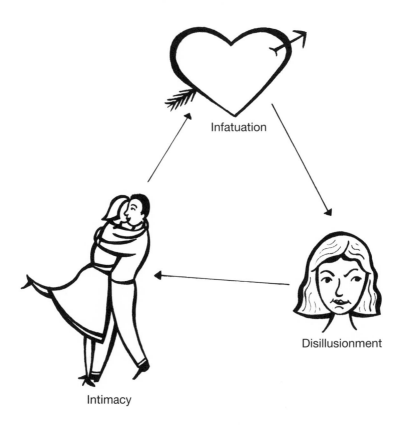

Infatuation

Disillusionment

Intimacy

Think back to the beginning of your relationship. Talk with
each other about a time when you moved from one part
of the cycle to another.

How is understanding relationship growth in this way helpful
to you?

The Difference between Forgiveness and Reconciliation

One of the discoveries Matt and Denise made was that forgiveness and reconciliation are not the same thing.

Forgiveness is the act of giving or receiving pardon for an offense. The offense can be something we do, what is called a sin of commission: an insult, a lie, washing her white sweater with your new red T-shirt. We are often unaware of the damage our actions do. Yelling might seem like a "normal" response to provocation; the silent treatment seems a richly deserved punishment. We also give offense through things we *don't* do—sins of omission: ignoring a spouse in distress, failing to follow through on a promise, forgetting an anniversary. In marriage we have plenty of opportunities to say "I'm sorry." Spouses intent on intimacy and covenant living will say "I'm sorry" many times.

In their book, *The Five Languages of Apology*, Gary Chapman and Jennifer Thomas suggest that forgiveness is made possible by one person apologizing to another with the intent to repair damage of some kind. They maintain that there are five aspects, or languages, of apology necessary for forgiveness. The first is expressing regret: "I'm sorry." The second is accepting responsibility: "I was wrong." The third is making restitution: "What can I do to make it right?" The fourth aspect is genuine repenting: "I'll try not to do it again"; and the fourth is requesting forgiveness: "Will you forgive me?" Their research suggests that although each aspect is important, people differ in what they need to hear before they are able to forgive the other. "I'm sorry" isn't enough for some people; they need to hear that the other accepts responsibility or that they will repent. In their book, they encourage couples to talk about what is needed to facilitate forgiveness between spouses.

It is also important that forgiveness be mutual. I sometimes see marriages in which one partner takes on the role of "apologizer." This leads to an unhealthy interpersonal dynamic that thoroughly distorts the mutuality of marriage. Both spouses do and say things (or forget to do and say things) that need forgiving. Both spouses need to ask for and grant forgiveness.

Reconciliation, on the other hand, deals not so much with specific acts that offend and require apology as it does with ongoing differences that cause hurt or irritation. The word *reconciliation* derives from the Latin *reconciliare*, which means "bring together again." This is the perpetual task of marriage. The work of achieving intimacy is the work of bringing together things that are not working or that have fallen or drifted apart. I would suggest that reconciliation is an essential element of creating an "us" from two "I"s.

Forgiveness involves repairing the damage our hurtful actions cause and then changing our behavior. Reconciliation has more to do with accepting each other's differences and using negotiation and compromise to address the hurt or inconvenience they cause. Every marriage has what psychologist and author John Gottman calls "perpetual problems" that cause hurt and disappointment (*The Seven Principles for Making Marriage Work*). He estimates that 69 percent of couple disagreements won't go away. Many perpetual problems stem from differences between personalities and tastes. Introverts and extroverts need to live with each other; so do sports fans and poets, artists and engineers, list makers and people who "go with their gut." All marriages have such unresolved issues.

But perpetual marriage problems can also involve quite serious matters. Husbands and wives often have very different ideas about child rearing, money, sex, and other significant issues. Many couples do not share the same religious beliefs. Profound differences in these areas rend the fabric of marriage, causing deep hurts that cannot be repaired by saying "I'm sorry."

What's needed instead is a workable process of reconciliation. This process involves continual and frank communication, a willingness to be flexible, skills in negotiating and conflict resolution, and, of course, a readiness to forgive. For such crucial work, many couples make use of marriage counselors and other professionals. But the essence of reconciliation is a spiritual transformation. Each partner must be willing to accept the other as he or she is, not as they want or imagine that person to be. This does not mean spouses stop encouraging one another to grow and change; it means their love is not conditioned on the change. Their love empowers the other to do the difficult work of making adjustments in his or her behavior. This is another way couples fulfill the promise they made on their wedding day to "honor" each other.

Reconciliation of "perpetual problems" is aided by prayer and the sacraments. Jesus repaired the relationship between God and the human family that had been torn by centuries of broken promises. And bringing unresolved differences and hurts to prayer is a couple's way of acknowledging that forgiveness is more than a simple act of the will on one's part. As John Monbourquette says in his book, *How to Forgive*, "Forgiveness stands at the crossroads between the human and the divine." It requires human action in addition to divine intervention. Because of the covenant God has made with us, we can ask for healing and reconciliation in our marriages when we are unable to bring it about ourselves.

Every couple has their own unique issues in need of reconciliation. For some, it is household habits that are irritating or messy. For others, personal behaviors are a source of frustration. One couple shared with me their experience of reconciliation around a particularly frustrating issue. She was very organized and kept a careful calendar of personal and family commitments. He kept most of his commitments in his head. As a result, they had many conflicts and last-minute changes of plans. She suggested, encouraged, and nagged him to write things down. He tried now and then but forgot most of the time. It didn't seem to bother him to change plans. After arguing for years, she acknowledged that she was the one bothered by this practice and she began taking his work schedule and finding out from him in advance about his commitments. She wrote them into the calendar herself and said nothing more. After experiencing the harmony and ease of operation that resulted, he eventually began filling in the calendar himself. Her willingness to change fostered his change.

Forgiveness and reconciliation can move a relationship out of disillusionment and into a mature acceptance of our spouse as he or she really is. Acceptance of ourselves is the other half of the equation. It takes humility to say, "I guess I do fly off the handle a lot" or "I do tend to be obsessive about the house."

Men or women who leave a relationship as soon as they have to face the flaws of the other are destined to remain in adolescence and never mature into intimate relationships. There is no way to get from infatuation to true intimacy without passing through disillusionment—by way of forgiveness or reconciliation of differences. We don't really know the person we married when we marry them; we carry around false notions of what this person is like. To really know our spouse, we have to give up these distorted ideas and see ourselves and the other clearly. We have to resist the temptation to make our spouse more like ourselves.

When we do this we expand our capacity to love. She loves him even with his fierce opinions, his snoring, and his tendency to speak before he thinks. He loves her with her hair products cluttering the shower, her long phone conversations with her sisters, and her habit of saying yes to anyone who asks for help. When couples do this, they manifest to one another an image of the God who loves them unconditionally and who forgives them readily.

Matt and Denise experienced the cycle of infatuation, disillusionment, and intimacy in their marriage. Soon after the wedding, each discovered that they had married someone who had flaws, flaws that could hurt them deeply. They talked openly and honestly without blaming, which helped each of them understand the hurt. Each asked for, and received forgiveness from the other, and also granted forgiveness when asked. This drew them closer together. Each time this happened, a bit of the old infatuation returned. I have noticed in older couples that if they have honored the unique and sometimes quirky things about each other and forgiven seventy times seven, they are even able to laugh at their differences, or at least smile when those differences emerge.

Developing habits of forgiveness and reconciliation, as Matt and Denise did, is an essential aspect of marital spirituality. The experience of forgiveness and being accepted and loved just as you are is a profoundly spiritual experience of God's presence in the world. Many couples find it helpful to set a time and a place where they regularly get together to talk over their differences. Sometimes it's necessary to learn new conflict resolution skills that aid in communicating about difficult issues or to read an article or book about forgiveness. When issues emerge that are difficult to resolve, many couples find that the sacrament of reconciliation helps to keep them honest about their own shortcomings. Reconciliation is holy work and is a pathway to intimacy in marriage.

How were forgiveness and reconciliation handled in your family of origin? How is your approach similar? How is it different?

What are some ways that you can let God's love and grace help you in your efforts to forgive and to be reconciled with your spouse?

From the Catechism

2844 Christian prayer extends to the *forgiveness of enemies,* transfiguring the disciple by configuring him to his Master. Forgiveness is a high-point of Christian prayer; only hearts attuned to God's compassion can receive the gift of prayer. **Forgiveness also bears witness that, in our world, love is stronger than sin.** The martyrs of yesterday and today bear this witness to Jesus. Forgiveness is the fundamental condition of the reconciliation of the children of God with their Father and of men with one another. [boldface added]

From the Gospels

But the tax collector, standing far off, would not even look up to heaven, but was beating his breast and saying, "God, be merciful to me, a sinner!" I tell you, this man went down to his home justified rather than the other; for all who exalt themselves will be humbled, but all who humble themselves will be exalted.—Luke 18:13–14

Then Peter came and said to him, "Lord, if another member of the church sins against me, how often should I forgive? As many as seven times?" Jesus said to him, "Not seven times, but, I tell you, seventy-seven times."—Matthew 18:21–22

So when you are offering your gift at the altar, if you remember that your brother or sister has something against you, leave your gift there before the altar and go; first be reconciled to your brother or sister, and then come and offer your gift.—Matthew 5:23–24

All this is from God, who reconciled us to himself through Christ, and has given us the ministry of reconciliation; that is, in Christ God was reconciling the world to himself, not counting their trespasses against them, and entrusting the message of reconciliation to us.—2 Corinthians 5:18–19

11

How to Deepen the Spiritual Connection
Nine Practices for Life Together

Good sacramental, covenant marriage doesn't just happen. You don't automatically become a good husband or wife simply because you want your marriage to succeed. In this chapter, we'll explore several practices that strengthen marriage and help it grow into a joyful and deeply spiritual union.

To have "practices" may not sound very romantic or spiritual, but marriages will not thrive unless both partners care about its well-being. The emotional, physical, and spiritual health of your marriage are inexorably bound together.

Keep in mind that God already dwells in your marriage in the ordinary duties and exchanges of everyday life. God is not simply with you; he is within you. You can experience the closeness with God described in the great prayer known as "St. Patrick's Breastplate:"

Christ with me,
Christ before me,
Christ behind me,
Christ in me,

Christ beneath me,
Christ above me,
Christ on my right,
Christ on my left,
Christ when I lie down,
Christ when I sit down,
Christ in the eye that sees me,
Christ in the ear that hears me.

This is your assurance. When you and your spouse set out to enrich your marriage, you can draw on the grace readily available to you in the sacrament of marriage.

God is certainly present in your marriage, and his grace is alive in your life together, but spiritual and marital growth requires that you act intentionally. To grow, you need to take positive, active steps.

Some of the advice that popular marriage experts offer for healthy relationships is very relevant to spiritual growth. A couple cannot build a life of communion if they cannot communicate. A covenant relationship won't be strong without good conflict resolution skills and the ability to forgive and be forgiven. Becoming a sacramental sign of God's love in the world takes human intimacy skills of honesty, vulnerability, and self-love. Marriage as a call to holiness requires self-sacrifice, a willingness to compromise for the common good, and mature interpersonal skills. A married partnership grounded in Christ is also a healthy, growing human relationship.

This chapter will review a number of ways that you and your spouse can tend to the spiritual and emotional health of your marriage. Some will appeal to you more than others. Some will seem easy to implement while others will appear difficult. Pay attention to your reactions to these ideas. The ones that attract you are probably areas of strength in your marriage. Begin there, and build on the practices you already have. But also pay attention to ideas that seem unattractive and hard. These may well be spiritual disciplines that are opportunities for the two of you.

Through the lens of faith we see that marriage is a call from God to build a rich and meaningful life and that God's grace makes it possible. But marriage is also a choice we make every day. It is a school of love in which we are always learning something new. The following are some suggestions for how to keep growing in your ability to keep the promises you made on your wedding day. They will help you build as "us", a partnership of love and life that will enable you to recognize the strengthening thread of God's presence in life's fabric. When considering them, look for the movement of the Spirit pointing you toward the opportunities that you can most readily seize. It is important to remember that spirituality is something God is doing in us in the midst of daily routines; our task is to be awake to the movements of the Spirit of God in and around us.

1. Learn Something New

Bob and Carol belong to a book group that reads great religious literature. Dan and Claudia are taking dance classes. Paul and Joanne and three other couples meet every two weeks to read and discuss Scripture. Charlie and Mary Ann are working their way through a video course on time management.

These are a few examples of how couples are strengthening and enriching their marriages by feeding them with new ideas and new learning. The value of continuing education is well-known in the professional world. Wise employees make frequent use of seminars, in-service training, and workshops to improve their skills and expand their knowledge. Wise employers encourage this. The same is true in marriage and family life. New learning stimulates conversation, lessens boredom, and can provide skills for managing stress and difficulties. Studies have shown that first-time parents who prepare for their new role by taking parenting classes experience less stress and report more satisfaction than parents who try to figure out child rearing for themselves. Studies have also shown that couples who take seminars in communication skills are more satisfied with their marriages than those who don't.

Try to do something *new*. It's fine to watch television together, go to movies, and have quiet evenings at home. But these activities can become routine. Couples tell me that even though they live in the same house and raise children together, they gradually drift apart or become so engaged in their own interests that they don't experience being an "us." They don't enjoy common activities that renew their relationship. The new activity can relate to an issue you want to address, or it can simply be for fun, such as taking golf lessons, a course in Chinese cooking, or a class in ballroom dancing. Learn a new language. Enhance your computer skills—together. It's fine to pursue your individual hobbies and interests, but learning as a couple offers many benefits as well. Such experience feeds the "us" that you have created.

Discuss: What have you done together to learn something new? How did this strengthen your relationship?

What new thing might you do now or in the near future to grow together? (Suggestion: look up courses and classes offered at your local parish, community college, recreation department, YMCA, art center, or other organization.)

---

2. Pray Together

The covenant you made with God and each other on your wedding day isn't a one-time thing. That covenant promise requires an ongoing dialogue between you and God. Prayer is the dialogue that sustains and renews the marriage covenant. Praying together can provide guidance, comfort, and encouragement in the hard work of marriage. In his book, *In His Spirit*, Fr. Dick Hauser, SJ, suggests that prayer is "raising the heart and mind to God through the power of the Holy Spirit." Prayer is the essential language of the spiritual life. We pray individually, and we pray in our community of faith. We should also pray as couples.

Couples pray together in any number of ways. Marital prayer can be somewhat formal—from a prayer book—or it can be an exhausted "O God help us," raising hearts to God when faced with a child's crisis or a seemingly irresolvable conflict.

Couples most commonly pray prayers of petition. Married life presents a multitude of opportunities to ask God's help: with our relationship, our children and other family members, friends and neighbors, finances, health, and work. We ask God's wisdom about decisions we must make. We pray for success in school and at work. We pray for protection. These prayers of petition acknowledge God's presence and power in our lives. Asking God's help together is a powerful way to join our minds and hearts in times of worry and distress.

We also pray in thanksgiving. Our spiritual lives are enriched as we learn to approach God with gratitude. In his *Spiritual Exercises*, St. Ignatius envisioned God as the sun, whose blessings permeate the entire world as the sunlight bathes the earth. He also saw God as a fountain gushing forth an endless and inexhaustible flow of gifts. The response to such a God is thanksgiving. We petition God for what we need, and we thank God for gifts received.

Our prayer also includes contrition. No other relationship exposes our faults as much as marriage does. Married couples can find profound healing as they express sorrow for the ways they have fallen short, and receive God's forgiveness. It is easier to name our faults before God than before our spouse. Doing this in prayer may give us the courage to admit our limitations to one another and give us the grace to make changes that are necessary for growing in love.

Praise is the most generous of all prayers. We don't need to ask or thank, or confess. When we praise God, we simply acknowledge God's goodness, as when we acknowledge the beauty and wonder of God's creation. Praise is the easiest prayer, but the least common for couples. Praise emerges out of a deep awareness of the goodness and beauty around us. We praise God for the sunrise on the way to work, for the beauty of a child's first words, for God's presence in the comforting gesture of a friend. The practice of praising God can help couples recognize the good things around them, even when times are tough.

The urge to pray together doesn't come naturally to most married couples. It can be difficult to carve out time for prayer in the hectic pace of family life—how can we find time to pray when there's not enough time to tend to our basic responsibilities?—or so it seems. Couple prayer often is not a priority for many reasons. When couples at retreats talk about prayer together, they often admit that they feel uncomfortable praying together. They may have differing prayer styles; one likes to pray silently and the other out loud with music or singing. One may prefer formal prayers that are read from a book while the other is more spontaneous. Another issue is time. Couples with small children find it especially challenging to pray together on a regular basis. Their days are filled from morning to night with little private time for themselves. Many couples tell me they wait for their spouse to initiate prayer, and there is no clarity about who is responsible for remembering the time and getting started with prayer.

Couples who make prayer together a priority develop this intimate conversation with God by exploring ways of praying that suit both of them. They use prayer books or a version of the Liturgy of the Hours. Some pray spontaneously. Others pray using psalms and other Scripture passages. Or they use music and times of silence before God. They mix and match these elements into a way of prayer that expresses their unique style as a couple. One couple told me they use a version of Vespers prayer (the evening prayer in the Liturgy of the Hours) and after the Lord's Prayer, which is part of Vespers, they briefly, spontaneously mention specific prayer requests regarding family and friends.

You may find a way of praying that suits both of you or take turns praying in each other's preferred way. It's good to experiment. Practical Considerations for Couple Prayer, Appendix 2, can assist you in exploring ways to pray together.

In what ways are you already praying together?

Together do the prayer inventory in Appendix 2, page 193, and complete the exercises to help you find a way to pray together that works for both of you.

---

3. Tap the Power of Ritual

A good-bye kiss in the morning; a cup of coffee delivered to the bedroom; a rosary prayed in the car. Without being fully conscious of it, most couples develop rituals of connection or celebration during their daily routines. Rituals are actions performed in a prescribed manner that have symbolic meaning. Nations, communities, religious groups, and families all use rituals to strengthen social bonds and to connect to group traditions. An American presidential inauguration is a ritual that celebrates the founding ideals of the nation. A high school graduation is a ritual that affirms the community's support for the accomplishments of its younger members. Christmas Day for many families is a ritual celebration of the family's solidarity through a pattern of worship, gift giving, and a meal. Rituals are anchors in an ever-changing world.

Many couple and family rituals are habits that take on symbolic meaning over time. One widow I know said that one of the times she missed her husband the most was on Sunday mornings, when they had a ritual of drinking coffee and reading the paper together in the kitchen before they were fully awake. My friend said that in the months after her husband's death she would sit alone in the kitchen on Sunday mornings and feel his presence.

Rituals and traditions have the power to bond people together even when there is discord or stress in the relationship. There are seasonal rituals and daily rituals; ethnic and religious rituals. There are intimate rituals of touch and service of one another. At a gathering of couples discussing rituals, one woman shared that her husband put her bath towel in the dryer every morning and brought it to her warm when she stepped out of the shower. Rituals are as creative and unique as the couples who create them.

Couples can tap the power of ritual by consciously choosing symbolic actions that are uniquely theirs. One couple rakes leaves together one day in the fall and plants flowers on the first warm Saturday in the spring. This is their symbolic thanksgiving as a couple for their lovely property. Many couples have rituals to celebrate their anniversaries. Some go away for the weekend, no matter how tight the finances. A couple I know plants a tree or bush every year on their anniversary. They ran out of room on their property after thirty years of marriage, so now they donate a tree on their anniversary to a local peace forest. Rituals can be as simple as kissing your spouse in the morning before leaving for work. Or rituals can be complex. A military couple I know developed a ritual to help them cope with the disruption caused by the frequent moves in a military career. At each new house, while the moving van was still in the driveway, they would first unpack a box with family pictures and other objects with sentimental meaning. With these objects in place, their new life could begin.

Rituals enhance the spiritual communion of marriage. They honor and acknowledge the "us" that you and your spouse are creating. Rituals provide a way of being together that foreshadows the unity and belonging that we will have with God in eternity.

Name one or two (or more) rituals that you have as a couple. Describe how those rituals provide a feeling of unity or intimacy with each other.

How might you foster greater awareness of rituals in your marriage? What other rituals might you add during this current season of your life together?

---

4. Suffer Together

Suffering is part of life, and it will inevitably come to your married life. *How* you suffer matters greatly; suffering can drive you apart or it can draw you together.

No one in their right mind would choose to suffer as a way of growing close to their spouse. We tend to avoid suffering at all costs. When it happens, some prefer to toughen up and pretend that everything is fine. Suffering can be a bonding or alienating experience. The trauma of a devastating loss or illness can drive a wedge between spouses—it can and does destroy marriages. Couples who have suffered the loss of a child experience divorce at a much higher rate than the norm. Parents of disabled children are also at greater risk, as are couples who are afflicted with illness and serious financial setbacks. One couple I know had a baby with serious physical disabilities. The father fled from the pain of this situation by throwing himself into his work. He would not talk about his stress and disappointment and fears but walled himself off from suffering. Sadly, this couple's marriage ended two years after the baby's birth. By fleeing from suffering, the father fled from the marriage.

No couple has to face suffering alone. You don't have to flee from pain or pretend it is not there. Because you are a partnership and have a covenant with God, you can share these burdens with each other and with Jesus, who journeys with you in every hardship. Jesus Christ, who willingly accepted the most hideous suffering, gives strength and healing to those who ask.

To acknowledge that one is suffering requires vulnerability, honesty, and humility. Many think that being strong means denying the truth of the pain or sorrow generated by loss or unfortunate circumstance. A man married forty years told me that when he was diagnosed with cancer he refused to talk about it with his wife because he didn't want to worry her. After months of stewing in his own anger and depression, he accepted help from a friend of his who had been through cancer treatment. This friend taught him how to admit his vulnerability and describe his fears to his wife. Instead of responding with worries and fears, she offered support and encouragement, and he was at last open to receive those gifts from her. He confessed that in all their years of marriage, he and his wife had never been so close, so united in facing a difficulty.

Suffering is a challenge, and the challenges we face in marriage are opportunities. When things go wrong, we often lament "Why is God doing this to me?" If marriage is a vocation, a calling from God, we can ask instead, "What is God asking of me?" God is present in all parts of your marriage, including the hard parts. God is always reaching out to you, inviting you to know him better and share his divine life more fully. He invites but does not force any of us; we respond or not. In hard times as well as good, the question is: what is God calling me to do or to be in this situation?

By sharing our suffering with one another and acknowledging our dependence on God, we become more of one mind and heart. Our shared life grows stronger. As we enter into the paschal mystery with Jesus, our love is strengthened and becomes a light for others.

Discuss a time in your married life when suffering brought you closer to each other. What made that closeness possible?

What might get in the way of your bearing the burdens of life together?

What would help you in sharing each other's difficulties more deeply?

5. Learn to Let Go

One of the great challenges of marriage is the challenge of letting things go. We let go of people—children, friends, colleagues, and family members all come into our lives and go out of them. Circumstances may change, with jobs or living situations causing us to let go of a comfortable way of life. As we grow older, we must adjust to the diminishment of our physical abilities. Letting go gracefully is truly an art.

Many of these challenges are "life cycle" changes. When you marry, you give up the single life. This first surrender is often the hardest. The first five years of marriage are the most vulnerable years, the years that see the highest rate of divorce. Many newly married people struggle to let go of the old habits and privileges of the single life. Children come, bringing joy but also drastic changes in lifestyle. Parenthood itself changes over the years. Gradually you let go of your control over your children, and eventually they leave your home—a letting go that is a complex mixture of joy and heartache. As life goes on you let go of parents and friends, of your responsibilities at work. You let go of robust health or of the flexibility to spend as much money as you once did.

Letting go is a psychological as well as spiritual challenge. We come to understand that we can wholeheartedly and enthusiastically embrace our current role and circumstances while realizing that these will inevitably change. We learn to be flexible, holding lightly the roles we embrace and then later relinquish. An attitude of expectant hope helps us take on a new role. This same hope can help us when we must let go of that role and face new experiences and possibilities.

Couples react differently to the challenge of letting go, often causing further stress on the marriage. Husbands and wives may respond differently to a move, the arrival of a new baby, or an illness that causes limitations in activity. Retirement is another major life cycle event that triggers great difficulties when couples do not learn how to let go together. Anger, resentment, and emotional distancing can erode a relationship when one person in the marriage moves on to new life in a time of transition or change and the other cannot. A wife confided to me during a retreat break that she and her husband of thirty-nine years were growing more and more distant as a result of his mother's terminal disease and death. He was angry and unwilling to accept this painful loss, and his anger and inability to grieve and let go of his mother was destroying their marriage.

Sometimes all that is called for is patience on the part of the one until the other is finally able to move on. The larger community can offer assistance at these times; other mothers can help this one let go of the adult child, or other men can help the newly retired husband see the possibilities ahead more than the end of a career.

The art of letting go requires a certain spiritual detachment. This is an attitude that sees the things of this world not as ends in themselves but as ways to love and serve God. Detachment is at the heart of the spirituality developed by St. Ignatius of Loyola. His classic expression of this attitude is found at the beginning of the *Spiritual Exercises* in the First Principle and Foundation.

The goal of our life is to live with God forever.
God who loves us, gave us life.

Our own response of love allows God's life to flow into us without limit.

All the things in this world are gifts of God,
Presented to us so that we can know God more easily
And make a return of love more readily.

As a result, we appreciate and use all these gifts of God
Insofar as they help us develop as loving persons.
But if any of these gifts become the center of our lives,
They displace God and so hinder growth toward our goal.

In everyday life, then, we must hold ourselves in balance before all of these created gifts insofar as we have a choice and are not bound by some obligation.

We should not fix our desires on health or sickness, wealth or poverty, success or failure, a long life or short one. For everything has the potential of calling forth in us a deeper response to our life in God.

Our only desire and our one choice should be this: I want and I choose what better leads to the deepening of God's life in me.

Detachment helps us meet the spiritual challenge of letting go. We let go of what we're clutching, and with our open hand we reach for something new. Letting go together, even if it's not done simultaneously, can deepen a couple's communion with each other.

Discuss together: When and how you have experienced "letting go" in your married life? In what ways was it difficult? How has it strengthened your relationship?

What opportunities to let go do you have now or in the near future? How do you want to approach them?

Read again the First Principle of the Spiritual Exercises of St. Ignatius, on pages 175–176. What is most challenging for you about the Ignatian principle of detachment?

6. Yield to Each Other

You have different ideas about the little things, like how strong to make the coffee, how to roll up the toothpaste tube, and how often to wash the car. Most couples disagree to some extent on critical things as well, like finances, style of life, raising children, and so on. Because we often are attracted to and marry people of different personality and temperament, our marriages provide endless opportunities to negotiate differences. Part of that negotiation will include yielding to each other.

In Christian marriage, the work of forming a partnership of love and life is holy work. It is not a legal or business partnership, but a spiritual partnership meant to lead the spouses into communion with each other and with God.

Yielding to each other in the big and little things of life is part of achieving mutuality. If you have ever experienced mutuality, you know that it is one of the human person's finest achievements! Mutuality is built on the recognition that both you and your spouse are gifted people. It requires that each of you respect the other, not only as equal partners in the great enterprise of marriage, but as friends on the same team in life. (That is why the other practices mentioned here like praying together, having common interests, taking time for play, and other activities are so important—they deepen friendship, a prerequisite for mutuality.)

It's important that yielding be mutual. As Paul reminds us in the letter to the Ephesians, "Be subject to one another out of reverence for Christ" (Ephesians 5:21). Both spouses must be willing to yield. The goal is unity, and you don't create a vibrant common life if you give way out of fear or exhaustion.

Yielding in marriage is directly related to the wedding vows to love and honor one another. Yielding is part of honoring a spouse's opinion and tastes; it is an expression of unconditional love for better or worse.

Most couples have a few unwritten rules they observe in yielding to each other. When it comes to her work's social events, he always says yes because he knows this is important for her career. When it comes to his ball games, she tries to attend most of them since he counts on her support and presence when he is competing. Some couples "take turns" having their say on household decisions. In the hard and fast decisions about how to discipline kids and how much money to spend on a car, a more sophisticated process of resolving conflicts is necessary—yielding is itself a part of any conflict resolution. Many marriage education courses include information on how to come to a common agreement when issues are deadlocked.

Interestingly, the marital research done by noted marriage researcher John Gottman suggests that men have a harder time yielding to women than women to men. Unity in marriage can never be achieved by just one person; the art of mutuality in marriage is a dance—it takes two.

And this is one more area in which the patterns in our families of origin will have a significant influence. If you came from a family in which one parent always yielded and the other always dominated, then you must be especially aware of how you live out the practice of yielding. Unity in marriage depends upon both people learning to yield sometimes and learning to lead sometimes.

Yielding requires a strong sense of self and a deep desire for unity. Without these qualities, it's very difficult to compromise and to negotiate differences. To yield means to give up, and we often experience this as a loss. Yet we "give up" because we deeply desire the unity that comes from that practice. Yes, we give up something, but in return we gain a shared life that is richer than the life we would have on our own. Through giving up we grow in our capacity to love. The act of yielding turns out to be a deeply creative spiritual act; it gives birth to something beautiful that did not exist before.

How have the two of you yielded to each other in your marriage, in big or small ways? How has this benefited you?

What would improve your ability to yield to each other in the future?

---

7. Find a Mission

There's a saying about love that pops up from time to time in songs and stories: Love isn't love until you give it away. The sentiment of this statement is profoundly true in a theological sense. The outstanding quality of God's love is that God gives love away. The Trinity of Father, Son, and Holy Spirit is a community of persons who love each other. We imitate this generous love when we share our love with our spouse. As couples, we participate in God's community of love as we reach out in love, beyond our marriage to others. We love our children. We love our family, friends, and neighbors. We serve our community. One of the best things we can do to deepen our love is to find more ways to give it away.

A Catholic marriage has a mission of its own in the world. Our wedding is a public ceremony, and we say our marriage vows before a community. The church blesses our union. Marriage is not a private affair; it is directed outward. Part of the mission of marriage is to form a community of love that gives and serves life in a way that manifests God in the world.

The mission of your own marriage changes over time. When you have children in your home, your primary mission is to raise them. This task bears profound social and spiritual consequences. One of the best things you and your spouse can do for your community is to bring up children who become responsible, productive, and faith-filled adults. Before children come and after they leave home, couples usually have more time to be involved in service outside the home. Some focus on caring for neighbors and family members in need. Others serve on a broader scale: parish work, nonprofit agencies, volunteer programs, local politics.

Some devote their missionary energies to national and international social justice efforts.

Your mission will be closely tied to your gifts. At baptism and confirmation, we are reminded that God created every person with gifts. Even gifts such as a sense of hospitality or humor are given for the good of the community. In marriage, we have the opportunity to nurture each other's gifts. One may be good at organization, the other at healing presence. All gifts are needed in the body of Christ, of which we are a part.

Often couples are able to serve together. One retired couple I know volunteers at their parish. She is a retired tax accountant and so advises the business manager on finances. Her husband had a career in computer technology; he's done wonders to update the parish computer system. One couple who are a doctor and nurse go to the Dominican Republic for two weeks every other year as part of a university outreach project.

Sometimes one partner's mission will be to support the other partner's work. A friend of ours has coached girls soccer for seventeen years. Her husband's contribution has been substantial but low-profile: he takes care of the equipment, drives the van, and organizes parent participation. He is in the background, but he and his wife take great satisfaction from doing a worthwhile volunteer service together. They and all other couples who serve others outside their home experience the paradox of St. Francis's prayer: "it is in giving that you receive."

How have you used your gifts as a couple for the good of others in your extended family and community? In what ways do you receive something back from that giving?

How have you each supported one another in using your individual gifts in the community?

Discuss your mission as a couple. What can you do to serve or continue to serve at home and in the community?

8. Learn to Receive

No marriage is an island. The journey through sickness and health, good times and bad, takes us to places where we need to turn to other people for help. Receiving assistance from those who love us is a way of experiencing the goodness and love of others. A friend's daughter gave birth to twins the day before her husband's business caught fire. They had two other small children at home. Without the help of family and friends, they could never have survived those first months with the twins. Others' kindness and generosity give us a glimpse of God's love.

Yet many people find it difficult to accept help. Many of us grow up in families in which self-sufficiency is a central value. We're told that a family should be strong enough to weather crises and meet needs without outside help. We can carry this attitude into our own marriages. Often we express this attitude by the discomfort we show when others offer to give us help. I'd rather shovel snow out of the driveway myself. I can get food on the table even though I'm sick with flu; I don't need a neighbor to bring dinner.

Our married lives are greatly enriched when we overcome these attitudes and gratefully accept the help we need. Sometimes our need is temporary: meals when a new baby comes, help with a home repair, emergency babysitting in a pinch, a ride to the store when the car breaks down. Even simple and fleeting help is meaningful when we receive it with a grateful heart. It opens us to others. It enlarges our community of love.

In times of trouble we need help of a more substantial kind. Every couple faces serious problems that they cannot solve themselves. We need help with finances, conflict resolution, child rearing, emotional problems. Many couples deal with alcoholism and drug addiction, infidelity, bankruptcy, and other serious difficulties. To weather such storms we may need the help of professionals and the support of good friends. We strengthen our marriages when we readily accept such help. What makes a healthy marriage is not the absence of such problems and conflicts—it's the way we address such problems.

Think of marriage as a journey; it's helpful to have other people along the road to give directions or a cold drink when you're thirsty. No one couple has everything they need for their marriage. In fact, you will put undue stress on your marriage very quickly if you expect that your spouse will provide—or is supposed to provide—everything you need in life. God created the marriage union; God also created the community in which such a union can thrive. But unless we are willing to be part of that larger community and receive others' help, we will run out of resources quickly.

Discuss your attitude about receiving help from others. Does it make you uncomfortable? Why, or why not?

When have you received help in the past? How did help received strengthen your marriage and family life?

If you resist receiving help, what might you do to help yourself be more comfortable with receiving?

---

9. Play Together

Most couples I meet are conscientious about their lives. They push ahead, day after day, week after week—working at careers, taking care of children, tending the home, socializing with family and friends, doing volunteer work. In fact, they take care of everything except the relationship itself. And when they do consider taking care of the marriage relationship, they are still in work mode. Often what the relationship needs, however, is not more work but more play.

Couples who want to remain friends need recreation time together. The word itself explains why it's important. *Recreation* comes from the Latin word for "restore." Recreation is not simply downtime, a well-deserved rest from pressure and stress. It is relaxation that restores something that once was there but isn't anymore. It's re-*creation*, a creative act that goes beyond merely ceasing activities.

In my many years of working with marriage education and retreats, most couples tell me that they simply don't take enough time to play together. They planned and enjoyed recreation before they were married and even before children came along, but in the childbearing years they had neither the time nor energy to plan recreation for themselves. Nor did they see a spiritual dimension to recreating together.

In the midst of work, family, and community responsibilities, play is usually left to the kids. Attending their games and playing with children is healthy play for a couple. But there is another dimension of play that deepens emotional connections between spouses and heals tensions and stress. Play is defined as something that is done for no reason but itself. It is purely for enjoyment and relaxation.

Time pressure is certainly a factor; so is the attitude that each person brings from his or her family of origin. Many of us grew up with the message that "play is just for kids" or "nobody plays until the work is done" (and the work was never done). If this is our thinking, then even the simplest recreation can feel like a waste of time.

But recreation has unique value for us. Stephen Covey, self-help guide and bestselling author, calls recreation the need to "sharpen the saw." He tells a fable of an encounter in the woods. A hiker comes upon a man who is sawing a tree with furious energy. The woodsman complains that he's getting tired and has been making little progress. The hiker asks, "Why don't you stop awhile and sharpen the saw?" The woodsman replies, "I can't do that. I'm too busy."

In the same way, we tend to keep working harder at our lives, even when we're not being very effective in our work or relationships. Sometimes a married couple needs to stop trying so hard, and to take the time to play. Play and recreation "sharpen" the relationship by building up friendship and strengthening the emotional bond between spouses. It is simply enjoyable—and joy makes marriage stronger.

Play can be simple: playing cards, taking a walk, or watching a regular sitcom on TV. It can get us out of the house: a concert, a trip to the beach, a baseball game. It can—and should—involve regular vacations. One couple, married seventeen years, has learned that even a short vacation helps. "We don't realize how wound up we've become," she says," until we've been off the normal schedule for a couple of days. It always helps our sex life, because so often we're both too tired and stressed to truly relax and enjoy ourselves." Studies of healthy marriages show that play builds up the friendship in a marriage and makes a huge deposit in the emotional bank account of the relationship.

Mark and Katie take a walk every evening after putting the children to bed (a neighbor comes over to stay in the house). Walking can be play. Sue and Tom keep a thousand-piece puzzle going and work on it together at least once a week in their few spare moments alone. Another couple tries to introduce something new into their sex life now and then in an effort to be more playful. Each couple creates their unique form of play.

The possibilities for creative recreation are limited only by your imagination. One couple who gardens together has hose fights when they've finished their work. They wear old clothes, knowing that they will be soaked when they're finished playing.

Play and recreation yield spiritual benefits as well. We can simply delight in each other when we take time away from the responsibilities of daily life. Our spouse is God's gift to us. Our marriage is a great blessing in our lives, a place in which God is present, a place of joy and contentment. We experience these blessings with special intensity when we have time to delight in each other, to laugh together, to taste once again the joy of being together that goes back to the simplicity of childhood. At such times, marriage can be what the Irish call "a thin place," where earth and heaven are not far apart.

In what ways do you play together at present?

Together work through the inventory and do the exercises on recreation in Appendix 3, page 197.

It's Up to You

For the past thirty years, my husband and I have been gathering with the same seven couples at a retreat house tucked away in a forest. We spend a weekend each year sharing family stories, playing games, counting our blessings, and grieving our losses. Over the years we have raised and married off children, buried our parents, and welcomed grandbabies.

The excitement that accompanies our reunion is always combined with amazement that we are still together! Each marriage is a unique combination of personalities, talents, and life experiences. Each contains a different history of good and bad times, strengths and limitations. The company of these friends and the experience of reflecting on our marriage journey as we are living it has been a rich part of our experience of God in our own marriage. I have observed that there are many good ways to do faithful sacramental marriage. There are some common pitfalls for couples as well as many time-tested skills and attitudes necessary for growing a healthy and holy relationship.

The opportunity of periodically taking a long and loving look at our marriage relationship, through the lens of faith in God's presence, has made a difference for my husband and me and for thousands of other couples. We do this in a somewhat unorganized fashion among friends, but there are many enjoyable and enriching opportunities for couples to reflect on their marriage in a more organized way. International and national groups such as Marriage Encounter, Christian Family Movement, Teams of Our Lady, and Marriage Retorno continually offer retreat weekends and small group resources for couples who want to grow in married love and commitment.

In addition to the company of married friends on the journey, the faithful practice of healthy relationship skills supports our efforts to live a committed sacramental life together. I hope you continue searching for resources and opportunitites to grow in those skills and in healthy attitudes toward friendship in the holy mystery of marriage. One excellent internet resource is a Web site from the U.S. Conference of Catholic Bishops: www.foryourmarriage.org.

True exploration into mystery never really ends. Our exploration into the mystery of marriage does not close with the final page of this book. I invite you to continue to take a long, loving look at your married relationshiop through the lens of faith—in God's steadfast covenant of love, which underpins your marriage covenant. Continue to discover, through thoughtful reflection and honest discussion, those circumstances and people through which God's love has clearly shown itself to you. Each day, ask yourself, Where can God's loving presence come to life in me—through acts of compassion, understanding, forgiveness, or the giving of myself?

Whether you do this alone, with your spouse, or with other couples, I wish for each of you the deep abiding pleasure of one another's company, the comfort and healing of sharing life's burdens, and the joy that flows from creating a life-giving partnership.

Appendix 1
Homemade Holiness for Married Couples, Based on Matthew 25:31–46

Corporal Works of Mercy	Spiritual Works of Mercy
1. Feeding the Hungry • shopping for groceries • cooking meals • stopping for fast food on the way to a game/meeting • packing lunches	**1. Instructing** • sharing information/skills with spouse • showing kids how to mow the lawn, clean, make things • establishing and enforcing house rules
2. Clothing the Naked • doing the laundry • shopping for clothing • polishing shoes, going to the dry cleaners, etc.	**2. Advising** • engaging in dialogue with spouse on important issues • helping children/spouse choose between options in their activities/work • gathering information for decision-making
3. Caring for the Sick and Imprisoned • going to the doctor, pharmacy, clinic • giving medications, wrapping sprains, etc. • taking temps, changing bandages, getting up at night • being with a loved one in the hospital or nursing home • trips to physical therapy	**3. Consoling** • being available to listen when spouse needs a sounding board • teaching children how to deal with loss/grief • affirming a spouse's efforts even when s/he doesn't succeed • cheering a child's team on even when they're losing the game miserably

4. Sheltering the Homeless	4. Comforting
<ul><li>working to make a house or rent payment</li><li>cleaning the house or organizing home duties</li><li>repairing, painting or other tasks that make a home livable</li><li>offering hospitality to visitors</li></ul>	<ul><li>listening to a spouse's work problems</li><li>holding a crying child</li><li>saying comforting things when something goes wrong (a failure or rejection)</li><li>caring for a sick loved one</li></ul>
5. Burying the Dead<ul><li>planning or going to wakes and funerals</li><li>cooking, babysitting or offering help to families when a death occurs</li><li>sending cards, flowers or remembrances to grieving families</li><li>cleaning out the home of a deceased parent or relative</li></ul>	
6. Welcoming the Stranger<ul><li>creating time and space for a new baby or grandchild</li><li>accepting a son or daughter-in-law (and his/her family) into the family</li><li>getting to know new families who move into the neighborhood</li><li>welcoming back relatives who have been estranged from family</li><li>accepting stepchildren</li></ul>	

1. *The spiritual and corporal works of mercy are the litmus test for followers of Jesus Christ. The pathway to holiness for married couples is lined with these routine activities. Place a check mark next to the listed activities you have done in the past two weeks.*
2. *Is it difficult to see your routine responsibilities as holy? Why? When you re-frame your daily service at home in light of gospel criteria for holiness, how does it change your attitude toward the duties of marriage and family? Explain.*

Appendix 2
Practical Considerations for Couple Prayer

Directions

Below is a list of personal preferences for prayer. Place a "+" next to those which you prefer, a "−"next to the ones you are not comfortable with and a "?" next to ones you are unsure about. After you have marked your preferences, share your list with each other and decide what methods and rhythms of prayer you will try in the future.

Ways of Praying

—— prayer with music

—— scripture reading

—— sharing reflections on scripture

—— prayer space with symbols

—— Christ Candle

—— periods of silent prayer together

——journaling

—— guided meditations

—— memorized prayer

—— Rosary/other devotions

—— Liturgy of the Hours

_____ variety of written prayers

_____ other _____

Kinds of Prayer
_____ prayer of petition (gimme)

_____ prayer of praise (wow!)

_____ prayer of contrition (oops)

_____ prayer of thanksgiving (thanks)

_____ meditation

_____ contemplation

_____ tevia prayer (spontaneous conversation with God)

Times for Prayer
_____ upon waking

_____ at breakfast

_____ at dinner time

_____ before bed

_____ every day

_____ three days a week

_____ other _____

Call to Prayer
_____ wife

_____ husband

_____ assign by week/day

_____ bell

_____ alarm

____ music

____ sunrise

____ sunset

____ other _____

Obstacles to Praying Together

Place a check mark next to the obstacles that apply to you.

____ am not convinced that it's important

____ am not sure God hears us

____ am not worthy to approach God

____ am angry or feel distant from God right now

____ am lazy

____ kids are always around, no privacy

____ am afraid of emotional intimacy that joint prayer demands

____ am angry at my spouse a lot of the time

____ don't have satisfactory prayer resources at home to use

Things I would like for us to pray together about:

____ kids

____ physical health

____ world situations

____ personal challenges/fears/desires

____ personal and family decisions

____ needs of friends

____ work issues

____ forgiveness

____ other _____

When you have discussed your preferences, complete the agreement below.

In the future, we will try the following ways of praying together: _____, _____, _____, using these kinds of prayer: _____ _____, at (*place time of prayer here*) _____. We have agreed that _____ will be responsible for calling us to prayer and that, when appropriate, we will agree to pray about the following _____ _____ _____ _____. An obstacle to praying together that we are willing to talk more about and do something about is _____.

Appendix 3
Recreation Inventory

Consider the power of play in marriage. Play is activity done for enjoyment, primarily for its own sake and perhaps secondarily to accomplish something.

Play deepens friendship, provides relaxation, improves relationship satisfaction levels, encourages laughter, strengthens emotional connections, reduces stress, and is fun!

Without talking to your spouse, check below the five play activities you would most enjoy doing together. Choose from the list and add your own suggestions. When finished, discuss your preferences and choose three activities to do in the next month. Fill out the questions below.

——— go to or rent a movie

——— attend a sporting event

——— go dancing or take lessons

——— go camping

——— play a card or board game

——— go bicycling

——— go for a walk

——— visit a museum

——— go stargazing or to a planetarium

_____ spend time at a park or beach

_____ visit a botanical garden

_____ take turns giving and receiving back rubs

_____ put together a puzzle

_____ attend a play or concert

_____ go horseback riding

_____ read to each other

_____ other _____

_____

We will try to do the following three activities in the next month:

1. _____

2. _____

3. _____

Who will initiate the play time?

When is the best time to play together?

What will be the biggest obstacle for us to overcome in being more intentional about play?

How will we remove that obstacle?

Selected Bibliography

Chapman, Gary, and Jennifer Thomas. *The Five Languages of Apology: How To Experience Healing in All Your Relationships.* Chicago: Northfield Publishing, 2006.

Doherty, William. *Take Back Your Marriage: Sticking Together in a world That Pulls Us Apart.* New York: Guilford Press, 2001.

Gaillardetz, Richard R. *A Daring Promise: A Spirituality of Christian Marriage.* New York: Crossroad Publishing Company, 2002.

Gottman, John M., and Nan Silver. *The Seven Principles for Making Marriage Work.* New York: Crown Publishers, 1999.

John Paul II. *The Theology of the Body: Human Love in the Divine Plan.* Boston: Pauline Books and Media, 1997.

Roberts, William P. *Marriage, It's a God Thing.* Cincinnati: St. Anthony Messenger Press, 2007.

Shivanandan, Mary. *Crossing the Threshold of Love: A New Vision of Marriage in the Light of John Paul II's Anthropology.* Washington, D.C.: The Catholic University of America Press, 1999.

Stanley, Scott. *The Heart of Commitment.* Nashville: Thomas Nelson, 1998.

Thomas, David. *Christian Marriage: The New Challenge.* Second edition. Collegeville, MN: Liturgical Press, 2007.

Waite, Linda, and Maggie Gallagher. *The Case for Marriage: Why Married People Are Happier, Healthier, and Better Off Financially.* New York: Doubleday, 2000.